"Everything that can be
invented has been invented."

— *Charles H. Duell,*
Commissioner,
US Office of Patents, 1899

IRELAND ON THE INTERNET

THE DEFINITIVE GUIDE

Written & Designed By
MICHAEL NUGENT

BLACKWATER PRESS

© 1995 Michael Nugent

Design & Layout: Michael Nugent

Cover Design: Mick O'Dwyer

Produced in Ireland by Blackwater Press,
Broomhill Business Park, Tallaght, Dublin 24

ISBN 0 86121 647 4

Dedication:

*To Barry Flanagan and Steve O'Hara Smith,
the pioneers of accessible and affordable Internet
services in Ireland for the individual user.*

Acknowledgements:

*To all who helped in any way in the production of this
book, including Anne Holliday, Steve O'Hara Smith,
Dermot McNally, Barry Flanagan and Colm Grealy.*

*Particular thanks to John O'Connor, Deirdre Bowden,
Anna O'Donovan, Philip Ryan and Eamonn Cooney
at Blackwater Press.*

To Mick O'Dwyer for the cover design.

*To Dermot McNally for technical proofing and
for suggesting the tempting alternative title of*
"Information Superhighway, My Arse".

*To Donal Harrington and Cliona Russell
at Ireland On-Line.*

*To the Internet Eireann Users' Group and staff
(particularly Dermot, Tony, Antóin, Barry, Feargal,
Johannes, Henry, Udo, Alex, Dave, Claire and Nick).*

*To the all-conquering Internet Lard AFC and to the
CREA-CPS mailing list contributors.*

*To Stephen Doakes and Ellena Byrne
for lending me my first Internet book.*

Michael Nugent was born in Dublin in 1961. He is a graduate of the College of Marketing and Design, Dublin, and a co-founder of the New Consensus peace group. He has completed a major study on the counter-screening of radiation through the use of lead oxide. In 1986 he was a candidate for the position of Irish national soccer manager. He currently has large phone bills.

In 1993 he co-wrote the number one best-selling *Dear John — The John Mackay Letters* with Sam Smyth. In 1994 he wrote *Dear Me — The Diary of John Mackay* with Sam Smyth and Arthur Matthews.

Home Pages ▶

Section A ▶

Section B ▶

Section C ▶

Section D ▶

Using this book

General overview

Contents

Acronyms — http://curia.ucc.ie/cgi-bin/acronym   The URL File

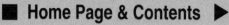

Introduction

By far the fastest growing area of communications technology in recent years has been the Internet. From two hundred computers in 1981 to over six million in 1995, it has consistently more than doubled in size every year and this growth rate shows no sign of slowing down. The technology itself is also constantly and rapidly changing, making any book about the Internet the literary equivalent of an opinion poll — a "snapshot in time" of what the Internet was like the day the book went to print. If you log on a week later, many thousands of extra words, images and sounds will have been added to this ever-expanding international archive of activity, opinion and information.

To tackle this challenge, *Ireland On The Internet* concentrates mainly on explaining — in understandable language — what you can do on the Internet. It includes the most comprehensive available directory of Irish Web pages (over 400 entries), a service and cost comparison between the main Irish Internet Service Providers, two free disks with free trial access to the Internet and various listings of places to go on the Net for information or fun. On technical matters such as the specific detail of how a particular software programme works, *Ireland On The Internet* will tell you where to find the most up-to-date information — either in other books or on the Internet itself.

This is also a guide for people who are simply curious about the topic. It assumes that you know nothing about the Net, and very little about computers. It avoids or explains "cyber-jargon", and is written so simply that even an adult can understand it. If you never want to look at a computer keyboard in your life, this book will give you a useful overview of what everybody else is talking about. Like the Internet itself, this book is ultimately about people, not computers.

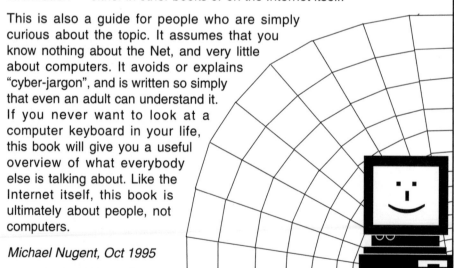

Michael Nugent, Oct 1995

What you can do on the Internet

More than you will ever find time to do. You can send ten letters by electronic mail to Carlow or Canada for less than a penny. You can search through marketing databases on a computer in California or add details of your own business for others to read. You can join in on five thousand newsgroups and discuss anything from antiques to zen buddhism. You can have a three-way online chat with your cousin in Australia and your friend in New York. And you can download free software to use on your computer to do all the above even more easily.

→ A1
Useful uses

→ A2
Fun uses

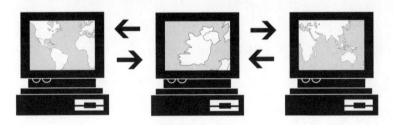

How to get yourself online in Ireland

There are several **ways to get online in Ireland**. If you have a computer and a modem, you can pay a privately owned online service for, among other things, limited internet access. Or you can go to a direct access provider, and get full Internet access for as little as £10 a month plus your phone costs. The dearest way is to rob a bank and buy your own personal permanent link to the net. The cheapest way is to work or study somewhere that has access, and spend all day on the Internet for free.

→ A3

→ C15
Main Irish Access Providers

Every day, **more of Ireland gets online**. Today you can read an online version of *The Irish Times* or *Hot Press*, download a Trinity College prospectus or the FM104 radio schedule, or send an email message to *The Late Late Show*, Pat Kenny or Gerry Ryan. In January 1995 there were over 45,000 Irish people with access to 6,219 Irish host computers linked to the Net. At a conservative estimate, there will be well over one million people in Ireland with Internet access by the year 2000.

→ A3

→ C13
Irish Web Page Directory

Amateur Astronomy — http://www.emoticon.com/emoticon/astro

The URL File

Finding what you want on the Internet

Here's how the **World Wide Web** works on the Internet. You call up a page of information onto your computer screen, called a "home page" if it is the top level page of a particular set of pages. Certain words on that page are highlighted. If you click on a highlighted word, your computer will bring you straight to a new page with further details on that topic. You will also find, on that new page, further links to get even more specific information on whatever topics are highlighted on that page. That means you are always reading whatever most interests you at any given moment.

→ B8

Finding what you want in this book

This book works in the same way. Certain words (particularly in Sections A and B) are highlighted, and have a page reference beside them. If you go to that page, you will find more detail on whatever topic that word refers to. Okay, so here you have to physically turn the pages and use real bookmarks but, hey, you gotta start somewhere. If you get lost, come back to this **Home Page & Contents** section.You can always find the information here to start you off again to wherever you next want to get to in the book.

→ Contents pages 12–13

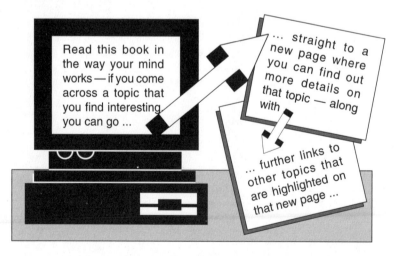

Read this book in the way your mind works — if you come across a topic that you find interesting, you can go ...

... straight to a new page where you can find out more details on that topic — along with ...

... further links to other topics that are highlighted on that new page ...

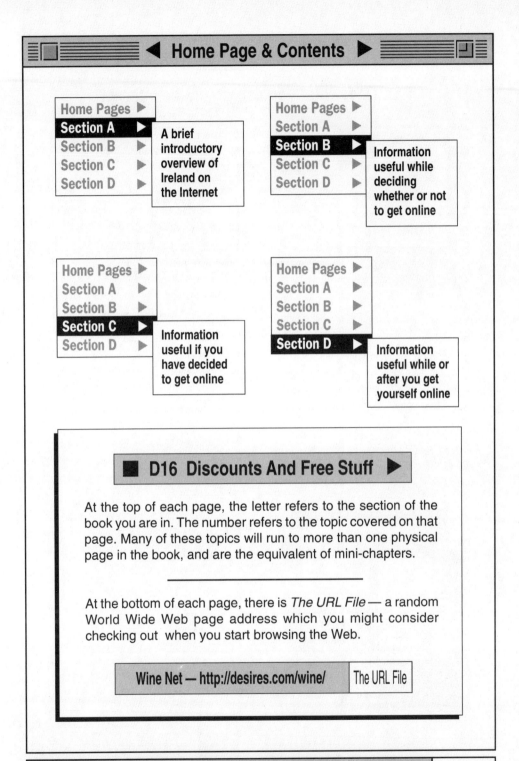

Home Pages ▶
Section A ▶ → A brief introductory overview of Ireland on the Internet
Section B ▶
Section C ▶
Section D ▶

Home Pages ▶
Section A ▶
Section B ▶ → Information useful while deciding whether or not to get online
Section C ▶
Section D ▶

Home Pages ▶
Section A ▶
Section B ▶
Section C ▶ → Information useful if you have decided to get online
Section D ▶

Home Pages ▶
Section A ▶
Section B ▶
Section C ▶
Section D ▶ → Information useful while or after you get yourself online

■ D16 Discounts And Free Stuff ▶

At the top of each page, the letter refers to the section of the book you are in. The number refers to the topic covered on that page. Many of these topics will run to more than one physical page in the book, and are the equivalent of mini-chapters.

At the bottom of each page, there is *The URL File* — a random World Wide Web page address which you might consider checking out when you start browsing the Web.

Wine Net — http://desires.com/wine/   The URL File

Animals — http://www.bev.net/education/SeaWorld/homepage.html   The URL File

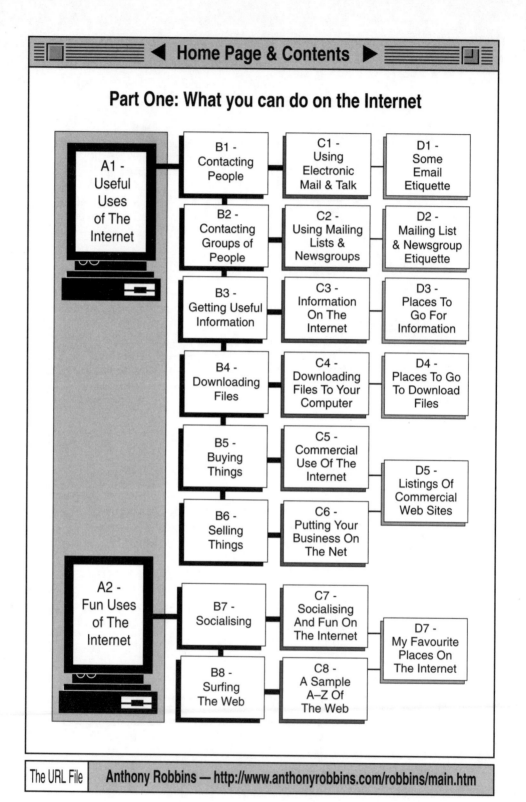

Part One: What you can do on the Internet

A1 - Useful Uses of The Internet

- B1 - Contacting People → C1 - Using Electronic Mail & Talk → D1 - Some Email Etiquette
- B2 - Contacting Groups of People → C2 - Using Mailing Lists & Newsgroups → D2 - Mailing List & Newsgroup Etiquette
- B3 - Getting Useful Information → C3 - Information On The Internet → D3 - Places To Go For Information
- B4 - Downloading Files → C4 - Downloading Files To Your Computer → D4 - Places To Go To Download Files
- B5 - Buying Things → C5 - Commercial Use Of The Internet → D5 - Listings Of Commercial Web Sites
- B6 - Selling Things → C6 - Putting Your Business On The Net

A2 - Fun Uses of The Internet

- B7 - Socialising → C7 - Socialising And Fun On The Internet → D7 - My Favourite Places On The Internet
- B8 - Surfing The Web → C8 - A Sample A–Z Of The Web

Part Two: The Internet and Ireland

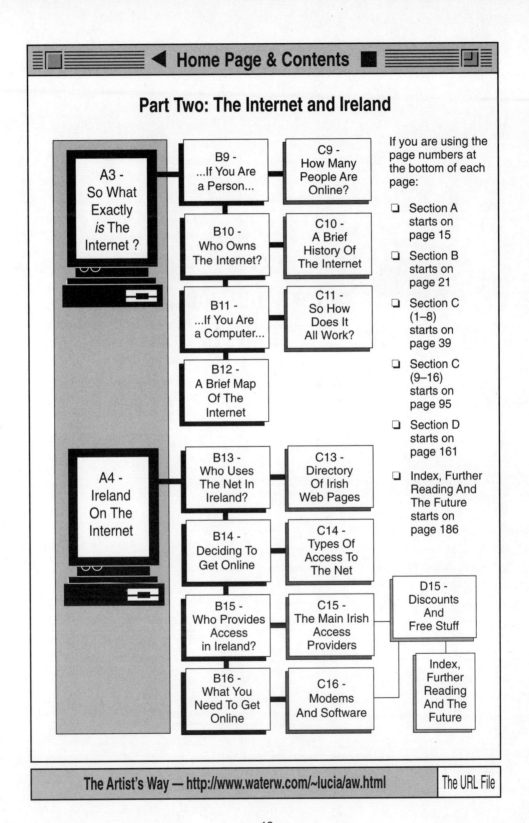

A3 -
So What
Exactly
is The
Internet ?

B9 -
...If You Are
a Person...

C9 -
How Many
People Are
Online?

B10 -
Who Owns
The Internet?

C10 -
A Brief
History Of
The Internet

B11 -
...If You Are
a Computer...

C11 -
So How
Does It
All Work?

B12 -
A Brief Map
Of The
Internet

A4 -
Ireland
On The
Internet

B13 -
Who Uses
The Net In
Ireland?

C13 -
Directory
Of Irish
Web Pages

B14 -
Deciding To
Get Online

C14 -
Types Of
Access To
The Net

B15 -
Who Provides
Access
in Ireland?

C15 -
The Main Irish
Access
Providers

D15 -
Discounts
And
Free Stuff

B16 -
What You
Need To Get
Online

C16 -
Modems
And Software

Index,
Further
Reading
And The
Future

If you are using the page numbers at the bottom of each page:

The Artist's Way — http://www.waterw.com/~lucia/aw.html | The URL File

The Internet is no more about computers than astronomy is about telescopes

— adapted from E. W. Dijkstra

Home Pages ▶

Section A ▶

Section B ▶

Section C ▶

Section D ▶

A brief introductory overview to Ireland on the Internet

Communication and information

You can use **electronic mail** to communicate instantly with the over thirty million people who have Internet connections. This is by far the most widely used facility on the Internet. You can subscribe to **mailing lists** and **newsgroups** which will allow you to communicate with many people simultaneously. You can search through thousands of databases of useful **information** stored on other computers and, when you find the information you want, you can **transfer** the file onto your own computer.

 → B1

 → B2

 → B3

 → B4

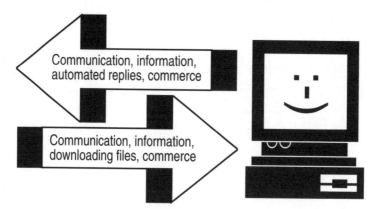

Communication, information, automated replies, commerce

Communication, information, downloading files, commerce

Online commerce

You can use the Internet to **buy things**. The details are stored, along with contact addresses or online order forms, on the pages of the World Wide Web. This is by far the fastest growing area of commercial activity on the Internet.

→ B5

You can also **sell things**. Set up your own World Wide Web site, and you can have your product or service information available to the public twenty four hours a day. When someone responds with a request for further information, you can have a computer set up to automatically respond to them.

→ B6

Internet commerce is in its infancy. It's not the mythical goldmine that some of the media hype would suggest. Nor is it anywhere near as insubstantial as the cynics would have you believe. It's certainly worth checking out before deciding either way.

| The URL File | **Australian Botanical Gardens — http://155.187.10.12/anbg/anbg.html** |

Socialising with other people

While many of the Internet's **mailing lists** and **newsgroups**  are devoted to business or academic topics, there are thousands more which cover virtually every imaginable specific interest; from antiques and beekeeping to computers and drama, from ecology and fashion to gardening and hiking, from intrigue and jobs to kittens and literature, from music and new age to oceans and poetry, from quotations and religion to science fiction and trivia, from the UN and vacations to works of art and x-rated stories, and from yoga to zen buddhism.

There are over ten thousand newsgroups alone so, whatever your interest, you'll find people who share it. And discussions that start on a mailing list or newsgroup can continue through private email between a smaller number of contributers. Obviously, you will use your own common sense in deciding whether or when you want to meet any of your new friends in real life.

Surfing the World Wide Web

If you have a quarter of one percent of an ounce of curiosity about anything, the **Web** is close to being the most fun you can → B8 have with your clothes on. Thousands of pages of information and pictures on every possible area of interest, with highlighted words that you can select to bring you to a new page with more details about that topic. It's growing fast, so it's a bit chaotic (actually, quite chaotic) (okay then, very chaotic) though there are a growing number of online directories that will guide you to the starting-off point of your choice.

If you are a person ....

The Internet is **over thirty million people** with whom you can share opinions, advice and information, and some of whom you can get to know as friends. There have already been

marriages which started out on the Net. It is a gardening club, a bible study group, a U2 fan club, a cat owners' advice group. It is a new set of communities, linked by common interest rather than just geography. It is useful and educational, and fun. It is not formally governed by anybody. Different people run different parts of it.

→ B9

→ B10

If you are a computer ....

The Internet is a network of **over six million computers** throughout the world. Each computer is itself part of a smaller network of local computers. The Internet is made up of over forty-five thousand of these local networks all linked together, and it is consistently doubling in size every year.

→ B11

→ B12

Computers are like Members of the European Parliament. They never make mistakes, but they cannot understand each other because they all speak different languages. To get around this, computers on the Net use a common language or **protocol** so that your IBM can "speak" to my Apple Mac.

→ C11

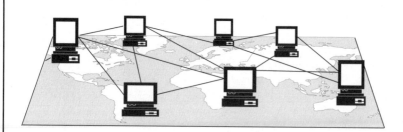

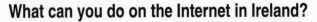
What can you do on the Internet in Ireland?

Readers, listeners or viewers who want to send a letter to *The Irish Times*, the Gay Byrne Show or the Gerry Ryan Tonight Show, can do so in an instant by electronic mail. Workers who want to collaborate on a joint business project with somebody in the next office and somebody in New York can do so by email and file transfer. Journalists who want to check up exactly what is in paragraph three of the Joint Framework Document on Northern Ireland can look it up on the World Wide Web. And anybody who wants to find a specific piece of information, play chess with somebody in China, or just browse through the many thousands of fun and useful pages on the Internet, can do so without moving a muscle (well, okay, so you have to move your eyes and your fingers).

→ B13

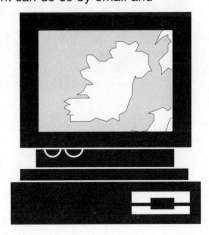

How do you access the Internet in Ireland?

Over 45,000 people in Ireland have access to more than six thousand host computers linked to the Internet. Many have access through a computer at work or in the college in which they are studying. Others have put themselves online directly from their own home — all that you need to be able to do this is a computer, a telephone, a modem, some Internet software, and an account with an Internet Service provider.

→ B14

→ B15

→ B16

You can get an account with an online service such as Apple's eWorld or the Microsoft Network, and get indirect access to many of the facilities available on the Internet. Or you can sign up with one of a growing number of companies that provide direct Internet access to individuals for as little as £10 a month plus the cost of your phone bills. And, regardless of where in the world you are contacting, you are only billed for the phone call to your Service Provider, which is usually a local call ...

Batman Forever — http://www.batmanforever.com/ | The URL File

The Internet is not a medium ... it's an extra large

— *Unknown*

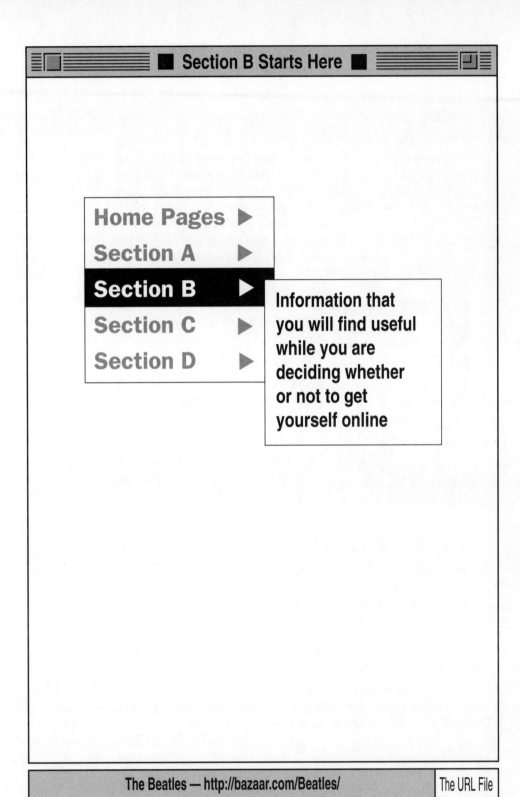

Home Pages ▶

Section A ▶

Section B ▶

Section C ▶

Section D ▶

Information that you will find useful while you are deciding whether or not to get yourself online

Sending an email letter

Electronic mail, or email, is the most widely used facility on the Internet. You may want to write to your brother in Australia. You type the letter on your computer, type in his **email address**, press the send button and, within seconds, the letter appears on his computer screen in Australia. How did it get there? It bounced from computer to computer around the world until it reached his computer. He can read your letter, type in his reply, and send it back to you immediately. If you are both online at the same time, it can all take less than a minute. If his computer is not online when your letter arrives, your letter will wait for him and will be there the next time he logs on and checks his **mailbox**.

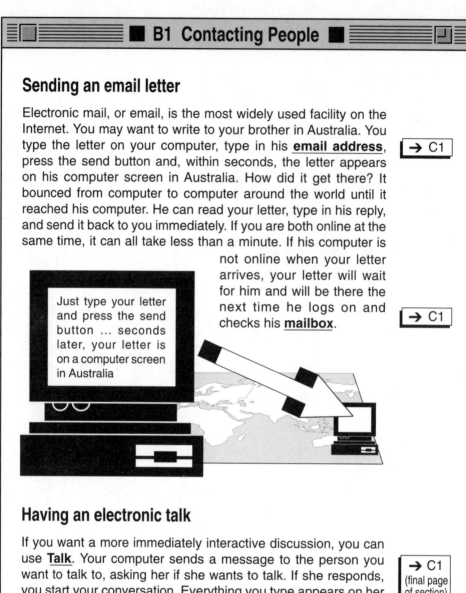

Just type your letter and press the send button ... seconds later, your letter is on a computer screen in Australia

Having an electronic talk

If you want a more immediately interactive discussion, you can use **Talk**. Your computer sends a message to the person you want to talk to, asking her if she wants to talk. If she responds, you start your conversation. Everything you type appears on her screen as you type it, and everything she types appears on your screen as she types it. If several people are online at the same time, you can have a group discussion, or **Chat.**

If you have a microphone and appropriate software on your computer, you can even have a real discussion, speaking and listening to each other's voices.

→ C1

→ C1

→ C1
(final page of section)

→ C7
(2nd page of section)

Subscribing to a mailing list

There are thousands of **mailing lists** on the Internet, where you can hold ongoing worldwide discussions with other people who have the same interests as you. A very popular mailing list will have many thousands of subscribers. One devoted to a more specific topic may have less than a hundred, but the discussion is likely to be more detailed. Subscribing is almost always free.

→ C2

→ C7
Sample
A–Z of
Mailing
Lists

Here's how it works. You send an email saying you want to subscribe to the list. When you next check your mail, you will find copies of every message that has been sent to the list that day from other subscribers to the list. If you decide to respond to one of the messages (or to start a new discussion yourself), copies of the message that you send are forwarded to the computers of every other subscriber.

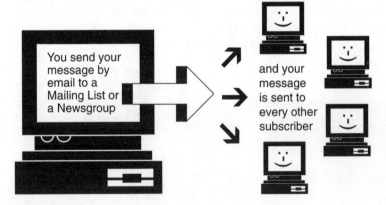

You send your message by email to a Mailing List or a Newsgroup

and your message is sent to every other subscriber

Subscribing to a newsgroup

If you subscribe to too many mailing lists, your computer can quickly become clogged up with thousands of messages that you'll never have time to read. So you can instead (or as well) subscribe to one or more **Usenet newsgroups**. Similar to mailing lists, and also free to subscribe to, newsgroups often have far more messages per day. Every day you check a list of the topic headings of all of the messages sent that day. You download and read the messages that sound interesting, and ignore the others. There are over ten thousand newsgroups.

→ C2

→ C7
Examples
of Usenet
news-
groups

Getting text-based information

The Internet has the equivalent of thousands of world-wide library archives that you can browse through by typing on your own computer keyboard. Most of the information is free, though there are some commercial information providers. When you are browsing for text-based information, a list appears on your screen of the folders that you can access on the computer you have logged on to. If you select one of these folders, you are given a list of the files (or other folders) within that folder. Eventually you reach the file that you want, and you read it. Or you can use programmes to **search** all available computers for a particular file, or for files containing a specific word.

→ C3

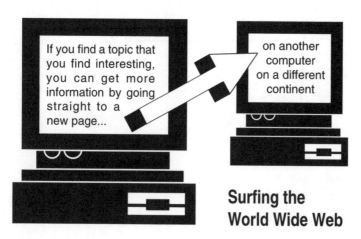

If you find a topic that you find interesting, you can get more information by going straight to a new page... on another computer on a different continent

Surfing the World Wide Web

→ C3
(final page of section)

→ C5

→ C6

→ C8
Sample A–Z of the Web

→ C13
Irish Web Page Directory

You can also use the **World Wide Web** to call up onto your computer screen a page which includes images as well as text. Certain words or images are highlighted and, if you select them, your computer will bring you straight to a new page with further details on that topic. You will also find, on that new page, further links to other pages, and so on, allowing you to "surf" endlessly from page to page. The first page you select might be on a computer in Dublin, the second in Australia and the third in Hawaii. Some pages also include sound and video, though — for most users — this aspect will remain relatively impractical until technology allows sound and video to be transferred faster.

The URL File | **Best Of The Web — http://wings.buffalo.edu/contest/**

Transferring files to your own computer

Once you have found a file with the information that you want, you may want to transfer it permanently to your own computer. If it is a file that you have already opened to read, you may be able to save it directly by using the save command on your computer. If it is a file that you have to transfer before you open it, you can use one of several programmes to do this. To download files, you also need to know whatever password the computer's owner has set for this purpose. However, there are hundreds of computer sites throughout the Internet which allow you free access to download their files using your email address as a password.

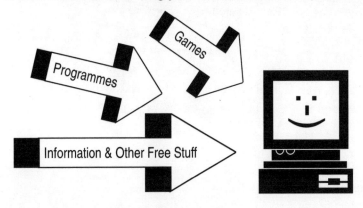

Free stuff — where's the catch?

For no cost you can download anything from information to computer games and even programmes — in fact, most of the programmes you need to use the Internet can be downloaded free once you have an Internet connection. Why is it free? Because the people who own the copyright are all certifiably insane. Another explanation preferred by my lawyer — much of the free information is on sites owned by educational or governmental establishments, many of the programmes or games are created by people who enjoy computer programming (and who allow you to use their creations if you send them a token payment of $10 or $20) and many of the free commercial programmes are test versions which have some features disabled but which allow you to try them out.

Looking for things to buy

The Internet has traditionally had a strong anti-commercial bias.
That has been changing rapidly in recent years. More people
are now online who do not share this anti-commercial bias. More
of the infrastructure of the Internet is now funded commercially.
And the impact of the World Wide Web in particular has literally
changed the face of much of the Internet. You will find relatively
few ads on mailing lists or newsgroups. But on the Web you will
find product information, offers of further details, and phone
numbers or online order forms for actual purchasing.
There are several directories which group
together commercial pages into single
online shopping malls. And
some companies offer
the equivalent of
online bank accounts,
which they hope will
eventually develop
into a system of digital
commerce.

One Unit of Digipunts, Redeemable at any Noddy in Toyland Store

→ C5

The dangers of online fraud

It is common knowledge that it is unsafe to transfer your credit
card number over the Internet, as malevolent but intelligent
fraudsters may hack their way into the transaction somewhere
along the line and find out your credit card number. You are far
safer writing your credit card number on a postcard where it can
be read without any computer hacking knowledge whatsoever,
telling it over the telephone to someone you have never heard
of, or repeatedly giving your actual card itself to any number of
shop assistants and restaurant waiters that you have never met
before. In other words, the threat of Internet credit card fraud
clearly exists, but no more so or no less so than in real life. If you
have been frightened by the media hype, there are several
methods being developed of online encryption of credit card
numbers — including Netscape secure pages and a joint venture
between Microsoft and Visa.

Suriviving commercially in the Internet age

If you don't have a presence on the Internet, your company will be left so far behind your competitors that right-thinking people will shun you in the streets as you make your way to the debtors' prison. Says who? Says the people who want to sell you your Internet presence. But that's just a coincidence. Surely.

Certainly, despite all the hype, your business can survive without an Internet presence. Equally certainly, an Internet presence can benefit your business, particularly in the medium to long term. More people can get more details more easily about your products or services. You can **automate responses** to requests for further information. You can allow people to **order online**. And you can get ongoing and instant **feedback** from your customers.

→ C6

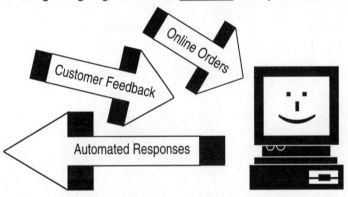

Creating a profitable Internet presence

However, you should follow a few **guidelines**, particularly if you are setting up a World Wide Web site. Currently, more people use the Web for browsing, entertainment and education than for business or research. So you should incorporate something entertaining or educational on your site. You should regularly update your Web pages with new material that will encourage a browser to return to your site repeatedly. And you should pay more attention to content than to particularly flashy graphics. These look great in magazine articles about the Internet, but large graphics can take several minutes or more to download onto the screen of many of your potential customers.

→ C6

Biorythms — http://www.qns.com/html/weborythm | The URL File

Mailing lists and newsgroups

As a rule of thumb, mailing lists usually have less people, and more detailed conversations, than newsgroups. Once you have tried out a few mailing lists, you might choose maybe two or three that you are going to participate most fully in. You will quickly find that you begin to recognise the names and attitudes and sense of humour and quirks of at least some of the regular contributers. Sometimes a discussion that starts on a list will continue off the list through private email between a smaller number of contributers. You can get to know some people very well. And sometimes members of a list who live close to each other will have a real-life get-together where you can put faces to some of the names.

→ C7
Sample A–Z of Mailing Lists

→ C7
Examples of Usenet newsgroups

Online games

You can also play online games. There are fantasy games in which the players take on different roles, quite often in new imaginary worlds. They participate by typing in the details of what their character is saying or doing. There are also email versions of popular board games like Diplomacy and chess. The players post their moves by email. A game of Diplomacy can last several months, with each player posting one set of moves every week. There are word puzzles, trivia games, card games. You can download one of many free computer games that you can play at home. And of course there are mailing lists and newsgroups devoted to discussing the tactics and strategies of playing specific games...

→ C7
(2nd page of section)

Caught in the web ...

The creation of the World Wide Web has made using the Internet much more enjoyable for the average non-technical common or garden human being.

→ C3
(final page of section)

While reading this, please substitute the topics mentioned with your own favourite areas of interest. You call up a football page which is full of information about the game in general, the World Cup, other competitions etc. You select a highlighted word that brings you to a new page about domestic leagues.

→ C5

→ C6

→ C8
Sample A–Z of the Web

A link from that page brings you to a page about the League of Ireland. You read a bit about the league, then see the email address of the Irish Football mailing list. You send a message asking to join the list, then select another new page about Shamrock Rovers. Obviously you're not interested in that as you have the intelligence to be a Bohemians fan, but you were curious to see what the page looked like (not too bad, actually).

→ C13
Irish Web Page Directory

From there another link brings you to the home page of the person who created that page. You find a list he has created of links to other pages he likes throughout the world, and before you realise it you're reading a page about somebody's favourite top ten films. Another link from there brings you to a page about the band that recorded the theme song of one of the films, where you can download an audio version of some of their music. From there you go to a page about the music industry in Britain.

Some time later, you decide to finish your browsing. Before you close down your computer, you check your electronic mailbox. An automatic response has arrived to your earlier email message, telling you that you have been added to the Irish Football mailing list. Already two or three messages from that list have arrived on your computer...

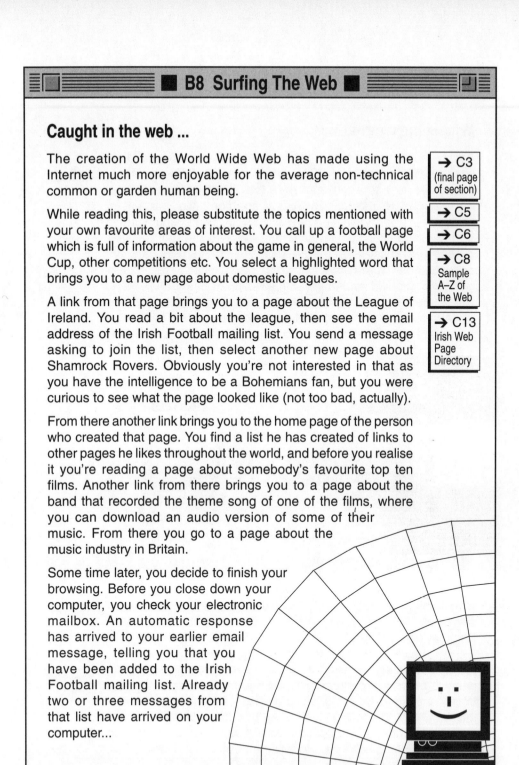

The Body Shop — http://www.bodyshop.co.uk/

The URL File

Who is the Internet?

From a human perspective, the Internet is a community of over **thirty million people**, all of whom can, at the very least, communicate with each other by email. Demographically, the average Internet user is male, white, north American and under 35 years of age. However, many millions of users, ranging from primary schoolchildren to buddhist monks, do not fit into this category. And these demographics are constantly changing as the Internet is repeatedly **doubling in size** each year. When posting to a public forum, like a mailing list or newsgroup, try to anticipate what may cause offence to people from different countries, continents and cultures than your own. That way, when you next find your mailbox clogged up with angry **flame** **mail**, you'll at least have the satisfaction of having intentionally offended the people who are annoyed with you.

Who is in charge of it all?

There are many types of organisation — academic, commercial, governmental and voluntary — that have varying degrees of influence on how the Internet is evolving. But no single body owns or runs the Internet — it is a large network composed of many smaller independent networks. A set of behavioural guidelines called **netiquette** (from *net etiquette*) has evolved over the years. Netiquette involves such things as keeping messages short to avoid wasting Internet resources, posting messages only to areas of the Net that are reserved for that activity, and trying to contribute to the Net community by, for example, helping new users to find their way around the Net.

→ C9

→ C9

→ D2

→ D1

→ D2

Who owns the transport system?

Nobody owns the transport system. Different people own different parts of it. And nobody owns the Internet. Different people own different parts of it. It is a network of computer networks, each of which runs independently of each other, and all of which co-operate with each other by using some of their resources to help transfer messages all around the entire system.

It's like going somewhere in real life. You get in your car, which you own. Or into a taxi, which somebody else owns. Or a bus, which might be owned by the government or a private company. You travel along a road that has built using taxpayers money. And cross over a toll bridge which is owned by somebody else. It gets even more complicated when you get to the airport and fly to somewhere governed by different people entirely.

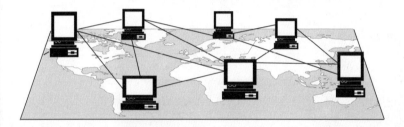

So who started it all off, then?

The Internet has quite an interesting **history**. It started out as a result of the US military defence budget being too big, and somebody deciding to spend the extra money on setting up a computer network. Eventually other independent networks joined up with this network, which evolved in an essentially unplanned manner into the Internet of today.

→ C10

It works best when people co-operate, but you can't insist on everything working out exactly as you want it to. Some people find this concept difficult to grasp, particularly when something goes wrong, because there is a rule that says that you have to be able to blame somebody when anything bad happens in your life. And it doesn't always work like that on the Internet.

Using telephones and roads

If I ring you up on my telephone, we communicate over one of the million or so telephone lines that are scattered throughout Ireland. Whether we are actually talking or not, nobody else can use the particular line we are using until we hang up. If the road transport system worked the same way, you would book one of the road routes from Dublin to Ballycastle, and nobody else could use that set of roads until you had finished your journey.

Just as the same road can be used by many different cars at the same time, the same cabling between computers on the Internet can be used to transmit many messages from many computers at the same time. The only limitation is the size of the actual line, which is expressed in **bandwidth**. All of which makes Internet communication — when it works properly — far more efficient in terms of resource usage than the normal telephone system.

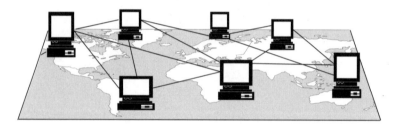

Moving house

You're moving house. One of your furniture removal vans might travel by one set of roads. Another may take a detour. A third may get caught up in a traffic jam. All arrive at different times, having travelled by different routes, but as you have labelled everything properly when packing it, it can all be sorted out. That's how computers transfer messages over the Internet. They break up the message into small packages, transmit each package by the most efficient route possible, then put them back together again in the right order at the other end. It's all controlled by a series of **protocols**, or agreed common communication rules, which allow you to lead a perfectly happy and successful life without knowing anything about them.

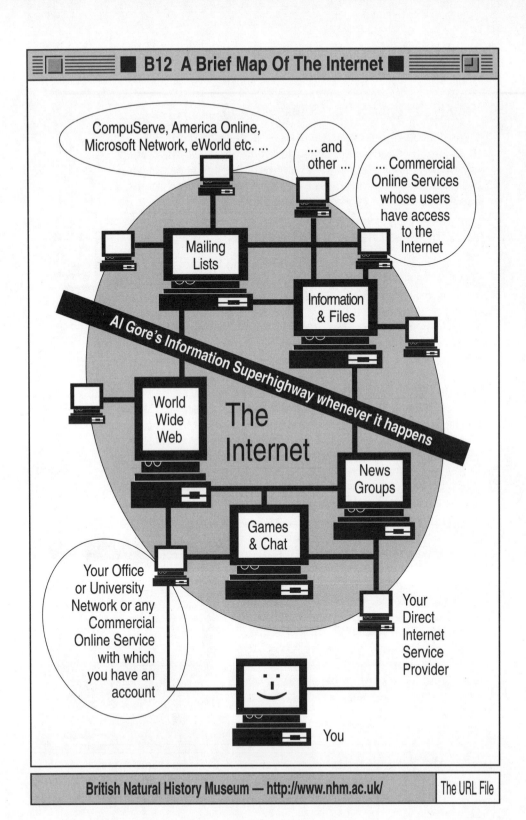

Who is the typical Irish Internet user?

Over 45,000 people in Ireland have access to more than six thousand host computers linked to the Internet. Of these, there is no typical user. People in Government agencies, businesses, research centres, universities, colleges, schools, and at home use the Internet for business and pleasure.

Who in Ireland has a presence on the Internet?

→ C13
Irish Web
Page
Directory

A random sample of Irish organisations who have put their own pages on the World Wide Web (for Internet users to access from anywhere in the world) includes ... 2FM, Abbey and Peacock Theatres, Aer Arran, AIB Group, Alliance Party of Northern Ireland, AMEV Insurance, Ancestral Videos, Anuna, Archeology Ireland, Ardagh Heritage Centre, Aubrey Fogarty Associates, Bailey's Original Irish Cream, Bank of Ireland Group Treasury, Barnardos, Big Issues, Biotrin International, Blarney Woolen Mills, Burren Fish Products, The Institute of Chartered Accountants in Ireland, Claddagh Films, Classic Hits 98FM, Dublin City Libraries, Dublin Gliding Club, Dublin Institute of Technology, Eleanor McEvoy, First National Building Society, FM104, Forbairt, The Forum for Peace and Reconciliation, Gerry Ryan Tonight, Goodbody Stockbrokers, The Green Party, Guinness, The HEA, HMV, Hot Press Magazine, The IDA, The Irish American Partnership, The Irish Times, Irish Trade Board, Kenny's Bookshop, Kinvarna Smoked Salmon, Knickerbox Swimwear, Militant Labour, Mitsubishi Computers, Mountaineering Council of Ireland, North Dublin National School Project, Northern Ireland Civil Service, On s'Amuse Toy Shop, numerous political documents, Premier Banking and Direct Insurance, Radioactive FM, Radio Caroline Dublin, Rathe House Equestrian Centre, RTE, most Regional Technical Colleges and Universities, The Ulster Historical Foundation, The Virtual Irish Pub, and many other businesses and organisations including ones which have been specifically established to work in the growing Internet area.

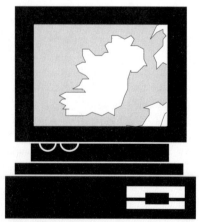

Types of Internet access

Many Internet users have accounts with commercial Online Services such as CompuServe and America Online. These services are themselves linked to the Internet, and their users can make use of that link. Other Internet users may work or study at universities, schools, businesses or governmental agencies which have computer systems that are linked to the Internet. And others may have their own personal link to the Internet, usually via a dial-up telephone account with an Internet Service Provider.

Dial-up Access: Your Computer telephones your Access Provider's Computer, using a modem.

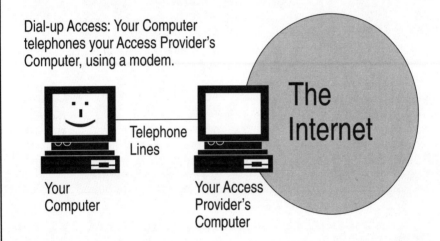

Telephone Lines

Your Computer

Your Access Provider's Computer

The Internet

What you can do with each

Partial access will allow you to use only some of the facilities available on the Internet. For example, you may be able to use email and read newsgroups, but not directly login to other computers or use the World Wide Web. **Full access** will allow you to use whatever Internet services you can access using the software on your own computer. You can get either partial or full Internet access by opening a **dial-up** telephone account with an Internet Service Provider. Or you can lease your own digital line and have **dedicated** or permanent Internet access.

→ C14

→ C14

→ C14

→ C14

Direct access to the Internet in Ireland

At time of writing, there were three main providers of direct Internet access in the Republic of Ireland (listed below in alphabetical order), with a fourth operating regionally in Cork and a fifth just being launched. Each has specific advantages which may or may not be important to you — to ensure that you get what you want, you should talk to each of them directly.

IEunet is based in Dublin, and is the Irish partner in Eunet, a Europe-wide network. It offers full access to the Internet and other related Internet services and — through joint ventures with other companies — is also part of *Cork Internet Services* and *Shannon Internet Services*.

→ C15

Internet Eireann is based in Dublin. It offers full access to the Internet, seven-day telephone support, and a flat rate charge with no limits for time online or data transferred. It offers World Wide Web and consultancy services. Internet Eireann was founded in August 1994.

→ C15

→ D15
Discounts and free stuff

Ireland On-Line, based in Galway and Dublin, offers full access to the Internet, online support, and a sales and consultancy service. It has local dial-up numbers in Dublin, Galway, Cork, Limerick and Sligo, with further access planned for other areas, as well as Northern Ireland.

→ C15
→ D15
Discounts and free stuff

Eirenet provides Internet services for individuals and businesses in the Cork region.

→ C15

HomeNet, the newest of the Irish Internet Service Providers, was launched just as this book was going to print. It is a subsidiary of the Horizon Computer group.

→ C15

As well as a computer, a telephone and an account with an Internet Access Provider ...

You need an internal or external modem

A **modem** is simply a device that allows your computer to communicate with another computer over the telephone lines. If your computer is a recent model, it may have an internal modem already built in. If it has not, you can buy an external modem, which you plug into your computer at one end and into your telephone socket at the other end. 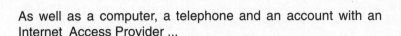 → C16

The faster your modem, the faster you will be able to transfer messages. Over time, this saving in phone bills can more than make up for the difference in cost between buying a slow or a fast modem. Currently, the speed of the fastest modem is 28,800 bits per second (often spoken as "twenty eight, eight"). This will cost you roughly £300. You can buy a slower speed modem, with which you can also access the Internet, for less than £100.

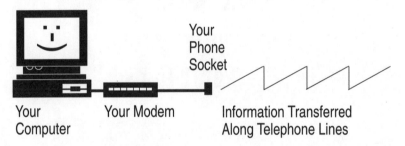

Your Phone Socket

Your Computer

Your Modem

Information Transferred Along Telephone Lines

You need Internet software

You need three types of Internet software. Firstly, you need communications software to enable your computer to contact your Access Provider's computer in the first place. Secondly, you need software to enable your computer to communicate with other computers on the Internet. Thirdly, you need application software to actually download your email or browse through Web pages. If your computer is a recent model, it may have some of this software already built in. And you can download a lot of other application software that you need, free of charge, from the Internet itself. → C16

6 This 'telephone' has too many shortcomings to be seriously considered as a means of communication. The device is inherently of no value to us **9**

—*Western Union internal memo, 1876*

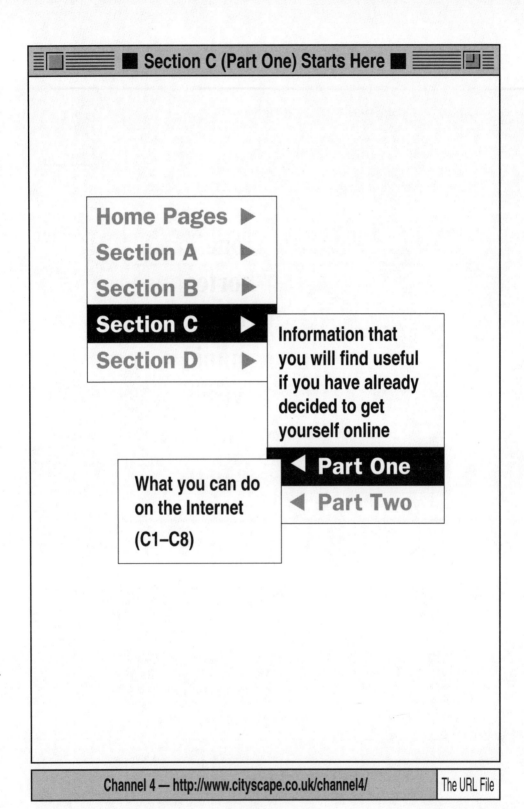

Home Pages ▶

Section A ▶

Section B ▶

Section C ▶

Section D ▶

Information that you will find useful if you have already decided to get yourself online

◀ **Part One**

◀ Part Two

What you can do on the Internet

(C1–C8)

Checking your mailbox for email

← B1
Sending an email letter

When you start up your email software you can check what mail has arrived in your mailbox. The layout will vary depending on the type of computer and software you are using, but the information on your screen could look something like this:

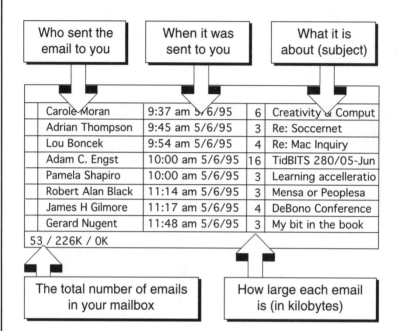

Who sent the email to you	When it was sent to you		What it is about (subject)
Carole Moran	9:37 am 5/6/95	6	Creativity & Comput
Adrian Thompson	9:45 am 5/6/95	3	Re: Soccernet
Lou Boncek	9:54 am 5/6/95	4	Re: Mac Inquiry
Adam C. Engst	10:00 am 5/6/95	16	TidBITS 280/05-Jun
Pamela Shapiro	10:00 am 5/6/95	3	Learning accelleratio
Robert Alan Black	11:14 am 5/6/95	3	Mensa or Peoplesa
James H Gilmore	11:17 am 5/6/95	4	DeBono Conference
Gerard Nugent	11:48 am 5/6/95	3	My bit in the book

53 / 226K / OK

The total number of emails in your mailbox

How large each email is (in kilobytes)

Reading and replying to your email

→ D1
Some email netiquette

You then highlight each message in turn and either open it to read it, or else delete it without reading it. After reading an email you can **reply** to it immediately, or forward it to someone else, or delete it, or save it to an archive file to reply to later.

When replying to an email (or sending a new email) you open a "new message" file. You type in the subject, the email address of the person you want to send it to, and your message. You can then either send it immediately, or else queue it to send later (it can be cheaper to send a batch of letters at the same time).

Addressing email for delivery

To send an ordinary letter to Bill Clinton, you must know his address (White House, Washington DC, United States of America). To send him an email letter, you must know his email address (*president@whitehouse.gov*). Everyone who is on the Internet has his or her own unique email address.

← B1
Sending an email letter

→ D1
Some email netiquette

```
Letters to the Editor,
The Irish Times,
D'Olier Street,
Dublin 1,
Ireland
```

email address:
lettersed@irish-times.ie

When the post office is sorting snail mail for delivery, they read the address backwards. First they check the country, then the city, then the road, then the house number, then the person's name.

Email addresses are also read backwards when being sorted for delivery. For example, *ie* tells us that it is an Irish address, *irish-times* tells us the name of the organisation, and *lettersed* tells us that it is to be sent to the letters to the editor page.

Reading an email address

There are at least three parts in an email address, and usually more. The address can include:

name of person @ name of computer (if any) .

name of organisation . type of organisation .

country code or top-level domain name

The name of the person is followed by an @ sign, and the other parts (called domains) are each separated by a dot (.) with no blank spaces between the word and the dot. Email addresses are traditionally written in lower-case letters, though this may not be technically necessary to have them delivered.

International domain codes

The last part of an email address is the country domain code — ie for Ireland, uk for the United Kingdom, jp for Japan and so on.

← B1
Sending an email letter

→ D1
Some email netiquette

Almost 100 countries have registered domain codes. The thirty countries with the most host computers (Ireland is 27th) are:

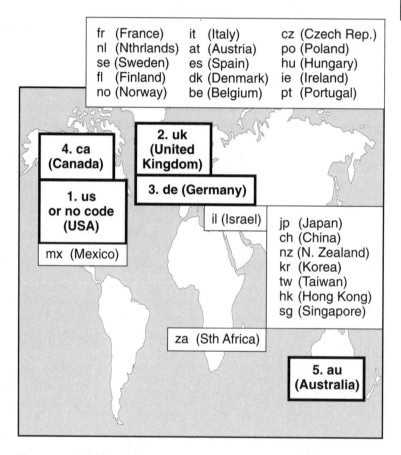

```
fr  (France)      it  (Italy)         cz (Czech Rep.)
nl  (Nthrlands)   at  (Austria)       po (Poland)
se  (Sweden)      es  (Spain)         hu (Hungary)
fl  (Finland)     dk (Denmark)        ie  (Ireland)
no  (Norway)      be  (Belgium)       pt  (Portugal)
```

2. uk (United Kingdom)

4. ca (Canada)

3. de (Germany)

1. us or no code (USA)

il (Israel)

jp (Japan)
ch (China)
nz (N. Zealand)
kr (Korea)
tw (Taiwan)
hk (Hong Kong)
sg (Singapore)

mx (Mexico)

za (Sth Africa)

5. au (Australia)

If an email address has no country code at the end, then it is probably a US address. As the Internet started there, US addresses didn't originally need a country code. Most US addresses end with the domain code for the type of organisation.

The URL File   Chocolate — http://www.godiva.com/recipes/chocolatier/index.html

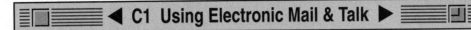
US organisational domain codes

The last part of most US email addresses is a three-letter abbreviation that tells you what type of organisation the email is being sent to. These domain codes are as follows:

← B1
Sending an email letter

→ D1
Some email netiquette

An address ending in...	Means that the organisation is ..
.com	**A US Commercial Business**
.edu	**A US College or University Site**
.gov	**A US Governmental Body**
.mil	**A US Military Organisation**
.org	**A US Non-Profit Organisation**
.net	**Someone Running a Large Network**
.int	**An International Organisation**

Other organisational domain codes

Some email addresses in other countries have similar domain codes just before the country code. For example, an address ending in *co.uk* is a UK commercial business, and an address ending in *ac.uk* is a UK college or university site — note that UK university addresses use *.ac* (academic) and not *.edu* (educational).

There is an educational network called *Bitnet*, which is linked to the Internet but which only uses *username@computername* for its addresses, with no other extensions. If you need to send email to a computer with a Bitnet address, try adding ".bitnet" at the end of the address. There are also other ways of sending Internet email to Bitnet addresses, which you will be able to check out once you are online.

Finding someone's email address

There are several online directories of people's Internet addresses, but none of them are in any way as comprehensive as the common or garden telephone directory. So the quickest way to find someone's email address is often to simply telephone the person and ask them.

← B1
Sending
an email
letter

→ D1
Some
email
netiquette

If they have ever posted a message to a Usenet newsgroup (which they are likely to have done), their name and address will have been recorded as their message passed through the Massachusetts Institute of Technology servers. Send a one line email message as follows: "*send usenet-addresses/(person's name)*" to *mailserver@rtfm.mit.edu*. The response will include a list of matching usernames, email addresses, and the date of their last posting. Here's part of the response to the request *send usenet-addresses/nugent*

```
hnugent@ix.netcom.com (Howard Nugent) (Apr 5 95)
GXSC07A@prodigy.com (Brian Nugent) (Apr 30 95)
tednugent@aol.com (Ted Nugent)  (Aug 15 94)
davidn@unique.pronet.com (David Nugent) (Aug 9 94)
Thomas J Nugent <tjnst9+@pitt.edu> (Aug 22 94)
prnugent@aol.com (PR Nugent) (Dec 26 94)
Wendy Holmes Nugent <GRHOLMES@ECUVM1.BITNET> (Feb 3 95)
davidn@csource.pronet.com (david nugent) (Jul 3 94)
mnugent@internet-eireann.ie (Michael Nugent)  (Jun 23 95)
T.Nugent@sct.gu.edu.au  (Jun 23 95)
```

There are also other programs — such as *Whois* and *Finger* — that will help you track down an email address.

Signing your email messages

Many people end their email messages with a signature that is the equivalent of a letterhead on the bottom of the page. This includes their name, their email address and sometimes their real-life address. Many signatures end up with a quirky quote from a book or a film. These signatures can be saved in your mailing or newsposting program, and can then be added automatically to whatever messages you post. If you are using an automated signature, try to keep it short — ideally four lines at most.

Using talk to converse in real-time

There are various programs on the Internet that allow you to communicate in real-time with somebody else. The most common and most useful of these is called Talk. To use talk, both people must have full Internet access. Both must also have the appropriate talk software. In practice, talk is not used very frequently on the Internet.

← B1
Having an electronic talk

→ D1
Some email/talk netiquette

If you want to talk with somebody, you send a request to her email address letting her know that you want to talk. A message then appears on her screen, giving instructions on how to reach you. If she responds, you can have a real-time talk with each other. Your screen will divide in two, with what you type appearing in one half, and what she types appearing in the other half. The same will happen on her screen, and you simply start typing.

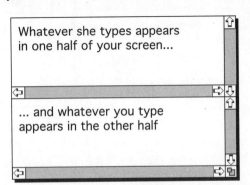

Whatever she types appears in one half of your screen...

... and whatever you type appears in the other half

Using IRC for a multi-person chat

There is also a facility called **IRC** (or Internet Relay Chat), which allows more than two people to use talk at the same time. Some business people use IRC as the Internet equivalent of a conference telephone call. It is cheaper than multiple long distance phone calls, and the conversations can be saved once the chat is over. In practice, however, chat is used far more regularly for recreation and fun than it is for business.

→ C7
(2nd page of section)

This may change in the future as the technology advances. Currently, If you have a microphone and appropriate software on your computer, you can have a real discussion, speaking and listening to each other's voices. There is also great future potential in area of Internet video-conferencing.

Cognitive Sciences — http://matia.stanford.edu/cogsci/   The URL File

Subscribing to a mailing list

A mailing list usually has three email addresses:

← B2
Subscribing to a mailing list

→ C7
Sample A–Z of mailing lists

→ D2
Group discussion netiquette

The subscription (or command) address	This is where you send email requests to subscribe to the list or to get other list information
The list (or discussion) address	This is where you send email messages that you want to be sent to everyone else on the list.
The listowner address	This is where you send email messages to the person who created the list or maintains it.

Always make sure that you send your list email to the correct address. For example, if you send a subscription request to the list address, copies of your message will be sent to hundreds of people throughout the world (all of the existing subcribers to the list). Of these hundreds of people, at least one will be sufficiently intolerant to send you a very impolite email asking you whether you have any brains and why you are clogging up their computer with *%!*@* email they don't want. Then you will start to cry and you will give up on mailing lists altogether.

Subscribing to a person-controlled mailing list

For any given list, the subscription address and the list address usually end up with the same words (as they are often two computers on the same network). But the subscription address will usually have the word "request" or "listserv" at or near the start of the address. If the subscription address has the word "request" in it, then the list is controlled directly by a person, who adds on new subscribers. You should send him or her a brief email message asking to add your name to the list. Include your name and email address.

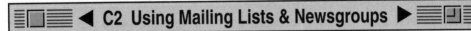
Subscribing to a listserv mailing list

A listserv (from "list server") is a computer programme that runs on an IBM mainframe computer. It automatically carries out the administrative functions of a particular mailing list. To subscribe to a listserv mailing list, you simply send a one line email message saying "subscribe (name of mailing list) (your name)" to the subscription address of the list (which will be listserv@something). You can shorten "subscribe" to just "sub". Don't write anything else, even please or thank you — the listserv, being a computer programme, will only be confused by your politeness. And who said computers are unlike people?

← B2
Subscribing to a mailing list

→ C7
Sample A–Z of mailing lists

→ D2
Group discussion netiquette

Other commands you can send to a listserv

You can also ask a listserv programme to unsubscribe you from a mailing list, or to send you details about the list, or to cancel your subscription for a period of time. Again, just send a one line email message to the listserv address. Some examples:

subscribe (list name) (your name)	**Subscribe to a list, or change your name if subscribed**
signoff (list name)	**Remove yourself from that list**
set (list name) nomail	**Stay on the mailing list, but stop receiving messages**
set (list name) mail	**Start getting messages again**
review (list name)	**Get a directory of subscribers**
conceal (list name)	**Hide yourself from review**
index (list name)	**Get a directory of list message archives, if they are kept**
help	**Get information on listserv commands**

The World's Top Ten Mailing Lists ...
Source: tile.net

1 David Letterman's Top-10 List

List address: topten@listserv.clark.net

You can join this group by sending the message "sub TOPTEN your name" to listserv@listserv.clark.net

Site: Clark Internet Services Inc, Ellicott City, MD, USA

2 The Mini-Annals of Improbable Research

List address: mini-air@mitvma.mit.edu

You can join this group by sending the message "sub MINI-AIR your name" to listserv@mitvma.mit.edu

Massachusetts Institute of Technology, Cambridge, MA, USA

3 TIDBITS — A Newsletter for Mac Users

List address: tidbits@ricevm1.rice.edu

You can join this group by sending the message "sub TIDBITS your name" to listserv@ricevm1.rice.edu

Rice University Information Systems, Houston, Texas, USA

4 ROADMAP — Internet training workshop

List address: roadmap@ua1vm.ua.edu

You can join this group by sending the message "sub ROADMAP your name" to listserv@ua1vm.ua.edu

University of Alabama, Tuscaloosa, Alabama, USA

5 NEW-LIST — New List Announcements

List address: new-list@vm1.nodak.edu

You can join this group by sending the message "sub NEW-LIST your name" to listserv@vm1.nodak.edu

North Dakota Higher Ed. Computer Network, Fargo, ND, USA

The URL File | **Computer Graphics — http://mambo.ucsc.edu/psl/cg.html**

... The World's Top Ten Mailing lists

6

OMRI-L — Open Media Research Institute
List address: omri-l@ubvm.cc.buffalo.edu

You can join this group by sending the message "sub OMRI-L your name" to listserv@ubvm.cc.buffalo.edu

Site: State University of New York at Buffalo, USA

7

INDIA-D — India News & Discussion
List address: india-d@indnet.bgsu.edu

You can join this group by sending the message "sub INDIA-D your name" to listserv@indnet.bgsu.edu

India Network, Bowling Green State University, OH 43403, USA

8

CCMAN-L — CND Chinese Magazine
List address: ccman-l@uga.cc.uga.edu

You can join this group by sending the message "sub CCMAN-L your name" to listserv@uga.cc.uga.edu

The University of Georgia, Athens, GA 30602, USA

9

LOOKING — Personals India Network
List address: looking@indnet.bgsu.edu

You can join this group by sending the message "sub LOOKING your name" to listserv@indnet.bgsu.edu

India Network, Bowling Green State University, OH 43403, USA

10

Public Access Computer Systems Forum
List address: pacs-l@uhupvm1.uh.edu

You can join this group by sending the message "sub PACS-L your name" to listserv@uhupvm1.uh.edu

University of Houston, Houston, Texas, USA

Reading and posting to Usenet newsgroups

Once there are over a couple of hundred people who want to discuss a particular topic, it can be more convenient to do so through a newsgroup. There are several differences between a mailing list and a newsgroup (apart from the fact that you need a separate programme to read newsgroup posts).

Firstly, it is easier to subscribe to a newsgroup. You don't have to send your name or address anywhere. You just add the name of the newsgroup onto a listing on your computer. Secondly, newsgroup posts are not sent directly to your computer. They are stored on your Provider's computer. You just check the list of subject headings and then download the posts you are interested in reading. Or, if somebody else is paying your phone bill, you can read them while remaining online.

← B2
Subscribing to a Usenet newsgroup

→ C7
Examples of Usenet newsgroups

→ D2
Group discussion netiquette

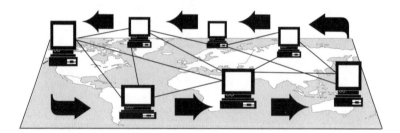

The newsgroup global merry-go-round

Newsgroups aren't owned by anyone, or stored centrally anywhere. When you send a post to a newsgroup, it joins all of the other posts that have been recently sent to that group. All of these posts then travel from network to network all around the world, with new posts from the subscribers to each network being added when the collection passes through that network.

This means that your message may appear instantly on your own network, in twenty minutes on a network in London and tomorrow on a network in Japan. It will stay on each network for as long as the administrator of that network chooses to allow posts to remain there, usually two or three days to a week.

Categories of newsgroups

Newsgroups are named the opposite way around from email addresses. The most general part of the name is at the front, and the most detailed at the end. So a newsgroup called *rec.arts.books* is most generally part of the *recreational* category of newsgroups, then part of the *arts* subcategory, and devoted to discussion about *books*. Or a newsgroup called *soc.culture.irish* is most generally part of the *social* category of newsgroups, then part of the *culture* subcategory, and devoted to discussion about *Irish* culture.

← B2
Subscribing to a Usenet newsgroup

→ C7
Examples of Usenet newsgroups

→ D2
Group discussion netiquette

A name that starts with ...	Means that the newsgroup is devoted to ...
alt.	**Alternative topics (see note below)**
comp.	**Computer related topics**
misc.	**Topics that don't fit in anywhere else**
news.	**Topics related to using newsgroups**
rec.	**Recreation, sports and hobbies**
sci.	**Topics in the established sciences**
soc.	**Topics related to social issues**
talk.	**Ongoing debates on politics, religion and other easily resolvable topics**

Note: The *alt.* category was created by popular demand after the original seven categories were established. Some sites do not carry the *alt.* category newsgroups, many of which can be trivial or tasteless or controversial. There are also other new categories, such as *biz.* (business topics), *bionet.* (biological sciences), *clari.* (a commercial news service) and *bit.* (various *Bitnet* newsgroups including some listserv lists).

The Usenet Newsgroup Categories ...

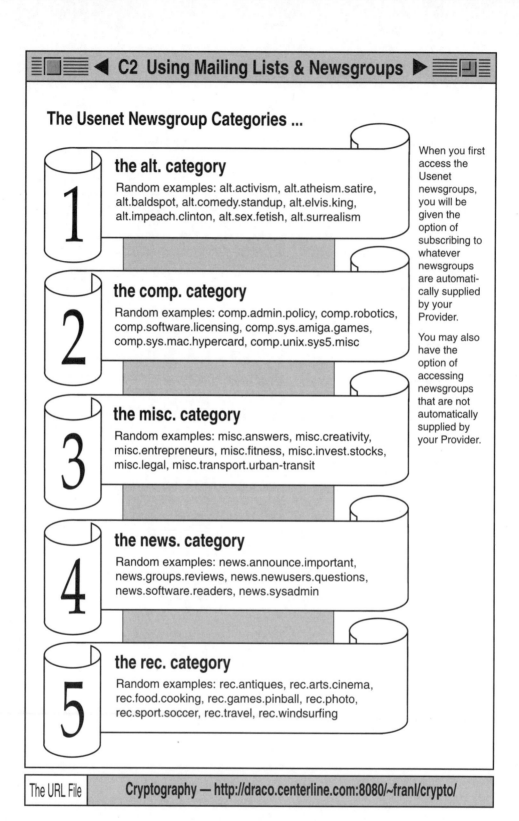

1 the alt. category

Random examples: alt.activism, alt.atheism.satire, alt.baldspot, alt.comedy.standup, alt.elvis.king, alt.impeach.clinton, alt.sex.fetish, alt.surrealism

2 the comp. category

Random examples: comp.admin.policy, comp.robotics, comp.software.licensing, comp.sys.amiga.games, comp.sys.mac.hypercard, comp.unix.sys5.misc

3 the misc. category

Random examples: misc.answers, misc.creativity, misc.entrepreneurs, misc.fitness, misc.invest.stocks, misc.legal, misc.transport.urban-transit

4 the news. category

Random examples: news.announce.important, news.groups.reviews, news.newusers.questions, news.software.readers, news.sysadmin

5 the rec. category

Random examples: rec.antiques, rec.arts.cinema, rec.food.cooking, rec.games.pinball, rec.photo, rec.sport.soccer, rec.travel, rec.windsurfing

When you first access the Usenet newsgroups, you will be given the option of subscribing to whatever newsgroups are automatically supplied by your Provider.

You may also have the option of accessing newsgroups that are not automatically supplied by your Provider.

The URL File	**Cryptography — http://draco.centerline.com:8080/~franl/crypto/**

... The Usenet Newsgroup Categories

6

the sci. category

Random examples: sci.anthropology, sci.bio, sci.chem.labware, sci.geo.meteorology, sci.nanotech, sci.physics.electromag, sci.skeptic, sci.stat.math

As one example of the relative availability of newsgroups, an Internet Provider might automatically supply you with 4,000 newsgroups divided as follows:

alt. 40% (approx. 1600)

7

the soc. category

Random examples: soc.college.teaching-asst, soc.couples, soc.culture.baltic, soc.feminism, soc.org.nonprofit, soc.religion.bahai, soc.veterans

comp. 15% (approx. 600)

misc. 10% (approx. 400)

8

the talk. category

Random examples: talk.abortion, talk.environment, talk.origins, talk.philosophy.misc, talk.politics.animals, talk.politics.soviet, talk.politics.theory, talk.rape

news., rec., sci., soc. and talk. 10% (approx. 400)

Others 25% (approx. 1000)

9

other categories

Random examples: bionet.organisms.zebrafish, bit.admin, bit.listserv.authorware, biz.books.technical, info.big-internet, k12.chat.elementary

Remember, there are over ten thousand newsgroups, and hundreds more have been added between the time this page was written and the time you are reading it. So there is almost a 100% chance of you finding a newsgroup devoted to your specific interests. And if not, you can always start your own.

CU-SeeMe — http://www.indstate.edu/CU-SeeMe/index.html

The URL File

Telnet, Remote Login and other fashionably futuristic terms that would not be out of place in Star Trek

← B3
Getting useful information

By using Telnet, or Remote Login, you can link up your computer to another computer, either in the building next door or on the other side of the Atlantic, and communicate as if your own keyboard and screen were attached directly to that computer. With some limitations, you can search through thousands of information databases, library catalogues and other information sources. The only snag is that, as you are "using" a different computer to your own, you may have to contend with a different set of commands and a different organisational structure than you have on your own computer. However, with a little time, effort, learning and experience, you should be able to use Telnet quite effectively.

With Telnet you must use whatever software is on another computer

With other search methods, you can use familiar software on your own computer

Easier ways of accessing information

If your life priorities do not include learning the commands needed to use Telnet, you can instead use software on your own computer to search for information in an easier manner. With programmes such as Gopher, WAIS and Archie, you can search for information using the familiar menu system you have on your own computer. With a browser for the World Wide Web, you can search through pages of text, graphics, sound and even animation by simply clicking your mouse on highlighted words to go to a new page.

Finding information with Telnet

← B3
Getting useful information

When you're using Telnet, the software that you are using on your computer is called the client software, and the software on the computer that you're linking up to is called the server software. Machines accessed by Telnet have their own set of commands, which are text-based and which you have to learn a bit about to use.

You start your Telnet software and type in the name of the remote computer that you want to access. You type in your name and email address if requested. Then you work your way through the data on the computer using the Telnet commands. Some computers have a menu-based system to help you find what you want. Others may just give you a % prompt. If this happens, you can type *?* or *help* to request help, or *ls* or *dir* to get a directory of files. When you are finished browsing, you type *quit* or *exit* to escape.

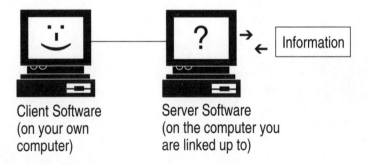

Client Software
(on your own computer)

Server Software
(on the computer you are linked up to)

What sort of information is available?

You can browse through over a thousand databases using Telnet. They include legal and educational databases, many library databases including the US library of Congress and the Shakespeare Database at Dartmouth Library. You can also use Telnet for Internet Relay Chat — the Internet equivalent of a telephone conference call — or for playing text-based games over the Internet. Also, if you have more than one account on the Internet, you can telnet from one account to another to, for example, check your mail.

Finding files with Archie

← B3
Getting
text-based
information

You may often be looking for a specific file that you know exists somewhere on the Internet, but you do not know where. You can find out where it is by using a piece of software called Archie (from the word "archive"), which gives you access to a database of the names of about 3 million files that are stored at known public archive sites. To put the scale of it into context, the current catalogue requires about 400 MB of disk storage.

You start up your Archie software, and ask it to contact the nearest Archie server (the database is stored in various server computers around the world, and you should generally first try the one nearest to you). You then type the name you are looking for. Archie will locate filenames which contain that string of letters. It will tell you the addresses of the computers on which it found the files, and the paths to the specific directories in which the files are stored.

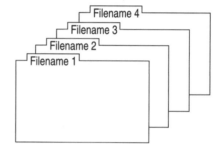

Filename 4
Filename 3
Filename 2
Filename 1

Archie will search
through filenames

Conducting an Archie search by email

← B1
Sending
an email
letter

You can also access the Archie database by email. Just send an e-mail message to an Archie server (the closest Archie server to Ireland geographically is at Cambridge and the address is *archie@doc.ic.ac.uk*). The message to send is:

> *path (your Internet email address)*
> *set search sub*
> *find (the name of the file you are looking for)*
> *quit*

For further details, send the message *help* to the same address.

Finding what's in files with WAIS

← B3
Getting text-based information

Archie will tell you where a file is on the Internet. WAIS (pronounced "ways") will help you to find information based on the words that are actually in the file. It has access to over 400 databases, containing everything from financial and educational information to weather details and Roget's Thesaurus. WAIS, by the way, stands for Wide Area Information Servers.

You start up your WAIS software, and type in the word or words that you are looking for, and select the database sources that you want WAIS to search through. Your WAIS software will then locate files in the requested databases which contain that string of letters. It will tell you where the files are stored. And it will rank the files that it has found according to the probability of their contents being relevant to the search you are making.

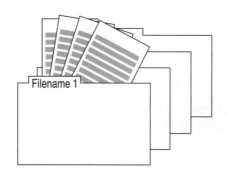

Filename 1

WAIS will search
through file contents

Conducting a WAIS search by email

← B1
Sending an email letter

You can also access the WAIS database by email. Just send an email message to *waismail@quake.think.com* using your regular email program. The message to send is:

> *search (the name of the database you want to search)*
> *(the name of the word or words you are looking for)*

When you get the results back, you can select the documents you want to read from among the ones it has found. Send another email message to the same address as follows:

> *retrieve (document ID as returned by WAIS search)*

The Dilbert Zone — http://www.unitedmedia.com/comics/dilbert/   The URL File

Finding information with Gopher

← B3
Getting useful information

→ D3
Ten top Gopher sites

Gopher combines, in one simple-to-use program, many of the things you can do with Telnet, Archie and WAIS. It also has other facilities, such as the ability to transfer files directly onto your own computer. And it hides all of the hard work from you.

You start up your Gopher software and select one of the many server sites for you to browse through. What you see is a series of menus. Each menu consists of a series of names, some of which represent folders or directories, and some of which represent files. If you highlight a filename, you can open it and read it or download it onto your own computer. If you highlight a folder or directory name, you can open it up and read the menu of its contents. You can keep burrowing deeper into the menu hierarchy until you find a file that you want. Or you can go right back up to the top of the hierarchy, and start burrowing through the files of a different computer instead.

Gopher will search files by hierarchy

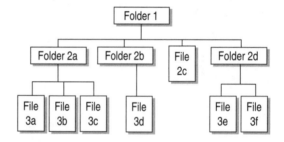

Searching gopher menus with Veronica

Veronica is a program that you can add on to your Gopher program. Instead of having to burrow through the various menu hierarchies of successive computers, you just type in a keyword and Veronica finds out if that file exists on any of the Gopher servers. This can be quite useful, as you could spend quite some time searching through the over 1300 Gopher sites, each of which has its own menu.

Veronica stands for Very Easy Rodent-Oriented Netwide Index to Computerised Archives. Seriously, it does.

The URL File | **Don't Panic, Eat Organic — http://www.rain.org/~sals/my.html**

Browsing information on the World Wide Web

← B3
Browsing
the World
Wide Web

→ D3
Ten top
Web sites
for useful
information

The World Wide Web is by far the easiest way of accessing information on the Internet. Firstly, it's not just words, but also pictures and even sound and video. It's amazingly useful and is the most intuitive and enjoyable by far of the many ways of searching for information on the Internet.

You start up your Web browser software, and type in the address of a page that you want to go to. Once you are there, you read that page. Some of the words or images on it will be highlighted, and if you click on a highlighted word or image, you are brought straight to a new page with further details on that topic. Any one page on the Web could be linked to up to ten or twenty other Web pages, some on the same computer, others on a computer half the world away. You can spend hours browsing through Web pages, constantly reading what most interests you at any given moment.

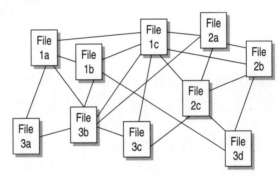

Files on the Web can have links to any other Web file

Searching for information on the Web

→ D7
Addresses
of Web
Search
Pages

There are several pages on the Web which include search mechanisms. One example is the WebCrawler database. Type in the address: *http://webcrawler.com/* and you will be able to type in any key word and have the software search the Web for references to the word. Or you can go to the page addressed *http://www.yahoo.com/* which has the most comprehensive topic-based directory on the Web. There are also commercial Web search services such as Infoseek, for which you must pay.

Transferring a file to your own computer

← B4
Down-
loading
files

→ D4
Ten top
FTP sites

Once you've found a file that you're interested in, you might want to transfer it permanently onto your own computer. If it is a file that you've already opened to read on your own computer (for example, a World Wide Web page), chances are you can transfer it by some variation of the *save* or *save as* command on the program that you are using. If it is a file that you have to transfer before you open it (for example, a software application program), you can use a process called File Transfer Protocol, or FTP.

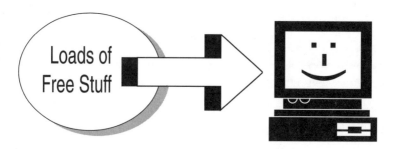

What is Anonymous FTP?

← B4
Free
Stuff —
where's
the
catch?

When you start up your file transfer software, and type in the address of the computer from which you want to transfer files, that computer will ask you for your login name and your password. This is one of the safeguards to stop everybody from being able to transfer files from everybody else's computer. However, at least 1300 known institutions have set up archives of publicly accessible files, where the whole point is that anybody can get at them.

The required username on these computers will usually be set to *anonymous* or *guest*. The password may be set to accept any text string, but you are often requested to leave your email address as your password so that the owners of the site can keep track of who has visited their site. Anonymous FTP is one of the most worthwhile and useful services available on the Internet. It's the process by which you can get what I like to technically label "free stuff".

Finding the file that you want

← B4
Down-
loading
files

→ D4
Ten top
FTP sites

Once you have got past the username and password stage, you might see a line that says "Guest login ok, access restrictions apply." This just means that the site has given you access, but you only have access to the files that are available to the general public. After that, you see a series of menus. Each menu consists of a series of names, most of which at the top levels represent folders or directories. If you highlight a folder or directory name, you can open it up and read the menu of its contents. You can keep burrowing deeper into the menu hierarchy until you find the file that you want to transfer to your own computer.

FTP files are stored in a hierarchical menu

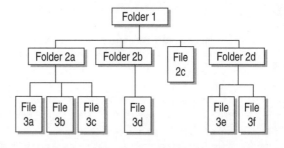

What to check before downloading a file

The first thing to check before you download a file is that you have enough disk space on your computer to store the file. If not, you may have to remove some of your existing files first.

The next thing to check is whether the file that you want to download is a *binary* file (as opposed to an *ASCII* file, which is a text file). Binary files will typically be software application programs, or picture or sound files, or files that have been compressed so that they take up less space (and time) to transfer. Most FTP programs have a command you can select to let the program know that the file you are transferring is a binary one. If you are not sure, select binary anyway. Most non-binary fles can be transferred in binary mode.

Types of binary files

Files stored on FTP archives have a three letter extension at the end of their names to let you know what type of file they are. Some common binary file extensions include:

← B4
Down-
loading
files

→ D4
Ten top
FTP sites

A filename ending in...	Means that the file is ..
.arc	ARK, PKPAK (PC compressed)
.arj	ARJ (PC compressed)
.bin	MacBinary (Mac encoded)
.cpt	Compact Pro (Mac compressed)
.dd	DiskDoubler (Mac compressed)
.gif	GIF (Mac or PC graphic image)
.jpg	JPEG (Compressed graphic image)
.lzh	Archive on PC or Amiga
.mpg	MPEG (Compressed animation)
.pak	PAK (PC compressed)
.sea	Self-Extracting (Mac application)
.sit	Stuffit (Mac compressed)
.voc	Soundblaster (PC sound)
.wav	WAVE (PC sound)
.zip	PKZIP/InfoZIP (PC compressed)
.zoo	Zoo (PC compressed)

The URL File   Edinburgh Fringe Programme — http://www.presence.co.uk/fringe/

Compression and extracting files

If a file that you download has been compressed, whoever put the file in the archive used a program (for example PKZIP or PKARK for PC files, or Stuffit for Macintosh files) to assemble various files together into one archive file, then compress it to a smaller size than the original files. You can use the same programme on your own computer to expand the file and extract the contents when you get it. The extension at the end of the filename should tell you what type of file it is.

← B4
Down-
loading
files

→ D4
Ten top
FTP sites

Encoding and decoding files

Sometimes a file that contains binary information will be converted into an ASCII text file using a process called UUEncode. This can be done using a programme such as WinCode for PCs. Another programme that encodes binary files to ASCII is BinHex for the Macintosh. When a file has been encoded, you do not have to use binary mode to transfer the file. So, for example, it could be sent to (and downloaded from) a Usenet newsgroup as well as an FTP site.

A filename ending in...	Means that the file is ...
.uu, .uud, .uue	**UUEncoded from Binary format to an ASCII text file**
.hqx	**BinHex (ASCII encoded for the Macintosh)**
.txt	**An ASCII text file**

If you open an encoded file as it is, you see a lot of nonsense text and what looks like Egyptian hieroglyphics. You can use a program on your own computer to decode (or UUDecode) the file in order to use it or see the picture it contains. Because UUEncoding a file makes it larger, files are often compressed before they are encoded. Which means that, after you decode them, you often have to decompress (or extract) them as well.

Dave Taylor's Internet Mall

In 1994 Dave Taylor did some research for a magazine article discussing commercial ventures on the Internet. His first Internet Mall listing — at the time the only public listing of commerce on the Internet — contained 34 companies and was 200 lines long. Today the Internet Mall has grown to a listing of over 1500 shops selling a wide range of products and services. You can access this listing on the World Wide Web by typing the following address: *http://mecklerweb.com/imall/*. You can then browse your way round the floors of the Mall and directly contact any company offering anything you are interested in buying.

← B5
Looking for things to buy

← B5
Dangers of online fraud

→ D5
Listings of Commercial Web sites

→ C13
Irish Web Page Directory

On this floor of the Mall...	You can browse or buy ...
Top Floor	**Food and Drinks**
6th Floor	**Furnishings**
5th Floor	**Clothes and Sports**
4th Floor	**Business Services**
3rd Floor	**High Technology**
2nd Floor	**Personal Items**
1st Floor	**Books and Media**
The Garage	**Autos**

Dave Taylor estimates that there are at least fifty thousand visitors every fortnight to the Internet Mall Web site, along with another thirty to thirty five thousand every fortnight who visit the Mall through other Internet services such as Gopher and Usenet News. This would equate to about six thousand visitors a day (to the Mall, not to any one particular site on it).

The URL File	**Enviroweb — http://envirolink.org**

What you can buy at the Internet Mall

You can get information on virtually anything, and the listing is very comprehensive (there is no charge for companies to be listed). The only services specifically excluded are multilevel marketing schemes, franchise opportunities, Internet service and access providers, other malls (they list the stores in the other malls instead) and computer consultants.

A typical entry is five lines of text, specifying who the company is, what's for sale, and how to contact them for more information. As the Mall tries to promote Internet-based commerce, they don't list postal addresses, phone numbers, fax numbers, or any other non-electronic contact information. If you see something you are interested in, there will be an email address or a World Wide Web address for you to follow up directly with the company offering the product or service. Some of the types of things you will find on the various floors of the Mall include...

← B5
Looking for things to buy

← B5
Dangers of online fraud

→ D5
Listings of Commercial Web sites

→ C13
Irish Web Page Directory

Top Floor	Food and Drinks	
Beverages	The Smoking Section	
Foods	Vitamins and Nutritional	
Sweets and Snacks	Supplements	

6th Floor	Furnishings	
Cooking and Kitchen Essentials	Indoor / Outdoor Decorations	
Furniture	Mobility and Disability Help	
Household Goods	Rugs and Blankets	

5th Floor	Clothes and Sports	
Clothes	Photographic Equipment	
Hunting and Fishing Gear	Sporting Goods	

All of the information on these panels can be found on linked pages from the World Wide Web page *http://mecklerweb.com/imall/*

4th Floor — Business Services

Accounting Services
Business Services
Email-based FAX Service
Employment Services
Finances and Banking
Freelance Services
Grant Proposals and
 Financial Aid
Insurance Companies
International Trade
Legal Services
Manufacturing Services
Marketing and Public
 Relations
Medical Information and
 Equipment
Monuments
Mortgaging & Home Loans
Net Banking

Personal & Family Learning
Pet Stores
Professional Training and
 Education
Real Estate
Relocation Services
Repair and Leasing Services
Research and Information
 Providers
Small Business Services
Speakers Bureau
Stocks and Investing
Telemarketing
Telephone and
 Telecommunications
Transcripts
Translation Services
Travel Agencies
Travel-Related Services

All of the information on this page can be found on linked pages from the World Wide Web page *http://mecklerweb.com/imall/*

3rd Floor — High Technology

CDROMs
CDROMs — Adult
Computer Fun and Games
Computer Network Solutions
Computer Peripherals and
 Other Neat Stuff
Desktop Publishing and
 Typeface Design
Educational Software
Hardware
Home and Office Software
Internet-Related Software

Media Duplication Services
Novelty and Custom
 Publishing
Online User Directories
Programmers Software
 Corner
Rentals and Used Software
 and Hardware
Scientific and Engineering
 Solutions
Support, Repairs and
 Upgrades

The URL File	Excuse Generator — http://www.dtd.com/excuse/html/exshom1.html

2nd Floor	**Personal Items**

Adult-Oriented Products	Health and Safety
Architecture & House Plans	Internet-Related Goods
Beauty and Personal Care	Jewelry
Collectibles	Kids' Stuff
Consumer Electronics	Matchmaker Café
(Stereo, TV)	Offbeat or Unusual Services
Counselling Services	Office Supplies and
Crafts and Hobbies	Stationery
Dental and Orthodontics	Online Repair Centres
Design Services	Optical
Entertainment and	Personal and Professional
Entertainers	Security
Environmental Wares	Promotional Goods
Florists and Other Plantlike	Seasonal Gifts and Crafts
Offerings	The Virtual Hardware Store
General Merchandise	Toys, Games and Novelties
Gifts	Weddings and Ceremonies

All of the information on this page can be found on linked pages from the World Wide Web page *http://mecklerweb.com/imall/*

1st Floor	**Books and Media**

Audio Books	Photo Album (Photographers
Books	and Galleries)
Business Bookshelf	Religious & Related Books
Electronic Books	Technical & Computer Books
Horror and Science Fiction	The Magazine Rack
Bookstores	The Virtual Art Gallery
Online Music Shop	Travel Books
Personalised Books	Video Connection

Garage	**Autos**

Automotive	Boats and Boating
Bicycles and Other Transport	Storage and Packaging

Celebrity Atheists — http://www.primenet.com/~lippard/atheistcelebs.html	The URL File

The Yahoo Business & Economy Directory

By far the most comprehensive directory of Internet resources is the Yahoo directory collection, which you can find on the World Wide Web at the address *http://www.yahoo.com/* . One of the Yahoo directories lists business and economy resources on the Internet, in over thirty separate subdirectories including:

← B5
Looking for things to buy

← B5
Dangers of online fraud

→ D5
Listings of Commercial Web sites

→ C13
Irish Web Page Directory

Current Business Headlines	Magazines
Business Directory	Management Info. Systems
Business Schools	Marketing
Classifieds	Markets and Investments
Companies	Miscellaneous
Consortia	News
Consumer Economy	Organisations
Economics	Products and Services
Education	Real Estate
Electronic Commerce	Small Business Information
Employment	Taxes
History	Technology Policy
Intellectual Property	Trade
International Economy	Transportation
Labour	Usenet

The Yahoo Companies Directory

To give an idea of the immense scale of the Yahoo business and economy directory, here are the numbers of companies in various business sectors that you will be able to get information about using the companies subdirectory. And remember, that's just using one of the over thirty Yahoo business subdirectories.

← B5
Looking for things to buy

← B5
Dangers of online fraud

→ D5
Listings of Commercial Web sites

→ C13
Irish Web Page Directory

Numbers of Companies in Yahoo Directory

Advertising (180)
Aerospace (89)
Agriculture (15)
Animals (56)
Apparel (171)
Architecture (60)
Arts and Crafts (338)
Auctions (12)
Audio (37)
Automotive (263)
Aviation (50)
Bed and Bath (8)
Biomedical (36)
Books (343)
Breweries (44)
Catalogues (18)
Ceramics (13)
Chemicals (39)
Child Care (8)
Children (10)
Collectibles (136)
Communications and
 Media Services (375)
Computers (4275)
Construction (82)
Consulting (188)
Conventions and
 Conferences (37)

Corporate Services (113)
Countries (194)
Demolition (1)
Disabilities (9)
Education (136)
Electronics (136)
Employment Services (179)
Energy (51)
Engineering (98)
Entertainment (382)
Environment (107)
Factory Automation (10)
Fax Service (15)
Financial Services (799)
Firearms
Flowers (90)
Food (274)
Funeral Homes (3)
Games (47)
General Merchandise (9)
Geographic Information
 Systems (15)
Gifts (161)
Government (13)
Health and Fitness (287)
Hobbies (61)
Home and Garden (124)
Imaging (35)

All of the information on the panel on left can be found on linked pages from the World Wide Web page *http://yahoo.com/*

 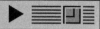
Numbers of companies in Yahoo Directory

Industrial Supplies (58)
Information (133)
Institutional Accessories (1)
Internet Access Providers
 (936)
Internet Consulting (274)
Internet Presence
 Providers (1423)
Investigative Services (25)
Investments (12)
Jewelry (85)
Languages (72)
Law (288)
Magazines (75)
Manufacturing (108)
Maps (24)
Marine (6)
Marketing (263)
Media (626)
Mining and Mineral
 Exploration (37)
Music (624)
Nanotechnology (3)
Networks (196)
News (340)
Newsletters (14)
Office Supplies (43)
Packaging (5)
Painting (5)
Party Supplies (4)
Performing Arts (2)
Photography (130)

Polls (4)
Printing (91)
Publishing (429)
Quality (15)
Real Estate (566)
Religion (11)
Research (58)
Restaurants (9)
Retailers (9)
Scientific (52)
Security (30)
Semiconductors (94)
Seminars (38)
Sex (176)
Shipping (32)
Shopping Centres (250)
Speakers (38)
Sports (431)
Technology Transfer (11)
Telecommunications
 (406)
Toys (22)
Trade (52)
Trade Shows (17)
Transportation (23)
Travel (574)
Trophies, Plaques,
 Awards etc. (5)
Utilities (28)
Vending Machines (7)
Warehousing (1)
Weather Information (14)

All of the information on this page can be found on linked pages from the World Wide Web page *http://yahoo.com/*

There is also a Yahoo business subdirectory that categorises specific products and services in a similar manner.

| The URL File | **Feminist Resources — http://www.igc.apc.org/women/feminist.html** |

The Yahoo Electronic Commerce Directory

Another interesting Yahoo business subdirectory is the one dealing with electronic commerce. The following is a very small sample of some of the Internet resources that you will be able to access from that page.

← B5
Looking for things to buy

← B5
Dangers of online fraud

→ D5
Listings of Commercial Web sites

→ C13
Irish Web Page Directory

Sample Yahoo Electronic Commerce Resources

Business and the Internet: discusses the history and future of the interaction between business and the Internet.

Buying via the Internet: participate in an online Academic Research Survey on shopping on the Internet.

Digital Money: several sets of Web pages devoted to this topic.

Electronic Auction: an online marketplace for wholesale inventory.

Electronic Commerce Association: regular seminars on topics such as electronic document management and commerce on the Internet. Discussions focus on the impact of available technologies on the way we conduct business.

Law of Electronic Commerce: The legal aspects of doing business without paper. Topics include electronic signatures, computer evidence and tax records of electronic transactions.

Marketer's Help Desk: Which size companies do best on the Net? Statistics, plus a listing of Net directories that you can use to promote your own site.

Marketing in Computer-Mediated Environments (paper): reports the empirical surveying of 290 commercial WWW sites.

The CAFE project: The CAFE (Conditional Access For Europe) project is a European Union ESPRIT project to develop a secure electronic payment system which protects the privacy of the user.

All of the information shown in the panel to the left can be found on linked pages from the World Wide Web page *http://yahoo.com/*

Acceptable Use Policies

The Internet consists of thousands of independent computer networks, most of which have their own policies as to what can and can't be done on their particular network. These policies are called Acceptable Use Policies. Some of these networks have very conservative policies, which reflect the origins of the Internet in the academic and research areas, which is why the Internet has traditionally had a reputation for having an anti-commercial bias. As an example, the American National Science Foundation, which controls the NSFNET backbone through which much Internet traffic has traditionally travelled, includes the following as part of its Acceptable Use Policy...

← B6
Selling things on the Net

→ D5
Listings of Commercial Web sites

→ C13
Irish Web Page Directory

Extracts from NSFNET Acceptable Use Policy

NSFNET services are provided to support open research and education..

..Communication with researchers and educators

..Communication and exchange for professional development

..Use for standards activities related to the user's research and instructional activities

..Use in applying for or administering grants or contracts for research or instruction

..Any other administrative communications or activities in direct support of research and instruction

..Announcements of new products or services for use in research or instruction, but no advertising

..Communication incidental to otherwise acceptable use, execept for illegal or specifically unacceptable use (i.e. use for for-profit activities, unless covered by the guidelines above), or extensive use for private or personal business

---

Acceptable Commercial Use

Other networks have emerged with Acceptable Use Policies that are far less restrictive for commercial use. For example, the Commercial Internet Exchange (CIX) was established as a non-profit trade association to ensure direct communication between commercial networks. In general, the trend is moving inexorably towards commercial use of the Internet being not only acceptable, but quite common. There are, however, some unwritten rules that you should abide by if you want to make life easier for yourself.

← B6
Selling things on the Net

→ D5
Listings of Commercial Web sites

→ C13
Irish Web Page Directory

... the acceptable face of capitalism on the Internet ...

Do NOT send unsolicited advertising

The reason that I've highlighted the word NOT in the above heading is that sending unsolicited advertising is by far the number one way of getting yourself into an awful lot of fuss and bother on the Internet. Yes, you can advertise. But do it in the right place. Do not mass-post unsolicited email to lists of people, and above all do not post advertisements to Usenet newsgroups (other than those specifically created for such purposes). I'm not saying this as a moral crusade, and they're not even my own personal views. But one reality of life on the Internet is that, if you send unsolicited advertising to a large number of people, your electronic mailbox will soon be deluged by increasingly hostile messages from not-very-polite people whose mission in life is to enforce the type of anti-commercial guidelines outlined on the previous page.

All right then, so where can I advertise?

The World Wide Web. This is the fun part of the Internet for users, so they will be in a better mood when they come to your ads. And, as they have to choose to come there (or stay there), a Web page advert cannot be considered unsolicited. Web pages, also known as Web sites, are what is generally meant when people talk about "having a presence on the Internet". They are created using a computer code called HTML (HyperText Markup Language) which — at its most basic — is about as complicated to learn as tying your shoelace. However, as Web pages are displayed differently depending on what programme is being used to view them, you should get somebody with some experience in HTML to either make up your Web pages for you or else train you how to do it yourself.

← B6
Selling things on the Net

→ D5
Listings of Commercial Web sites

→ C13
Irish Web Page Directory

Remember that any one of your Web pages can have links to any number of other Web pages...

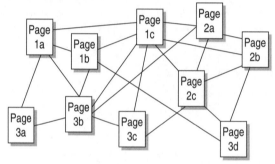

What should I put on my Web pages?

Don't think of your Web pages as advertisements. The Web operates in a very different manner than other forms of media. Think of your Web pages as interactive marketing forums, where you can give your reader information about your product or service, and also find out what she likes and dislikes about it. Think in terms of conveying actual information to one person as opposed to clever slogans to a crowd. Think visually, though not about very large graphics, which can take too long to transfer over the types of modems many of your readers will be using. Think about what links you can have on your page to lead the reader to other pages with further items of interest. And think about what else you can put on your pages to encourage people to return to them time and time again.

How do I advertise the existance of my Web pages?

You can't send advertisements to mailing lists or to Usenet newsgroups, but you can send short announcements about the existence of your Web pages — as long as the list or the newsgroup is relevant to the product or service you are promoting on your Web page. Keep it short, don't pad it out with hype, and highlight any useful service or information that is available free on your Web page. Ideally, include an auto-responder email address as well (see below).

← B6
Selling things on the Net

→ D5
Listings of Commercial Web sites

→ C13
Irish Web Page Directory

You can also get your Web pages listed — usually without any charge — in the directories of resources that are increasingly abundant on the Net. You can include your Web page address on your email signature. If your area of business can generate sufficient interest, you can start your own mailing list. And of course you can publicise your Web page address in any print advertisements you are placing in the real world.

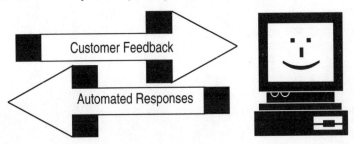

Customer Feedback

Automated Responses

Getting and responding to feedback

You can have forms included in your Web pages so that your readers can respond directly to you. And you can automate much of the process of responding to feedback, whether it be from Web pages or from announcements to newsgroups. This is particularly the case when responding to email requests for further information. You can have a specific email address, say *info@your.address*, where a computer programme will automatically take the address the request came from and post a pre-programmed response. This means instant additional information, often within thirty seconds of your reader requesting it, while you are relaxing drinking coffee and watching your favourite television programme at home.

An interesting little football story

← B7
Socialising
on the
Internet

The weekend before I wrote this paragraph, I went to watch a football match in Dublin, then retired to a local hostelry for some beverages with some friends from Ireland and England. Since you ask, Leeds beat Shelbourne 3-1 and the game was pretty average, though at least we weren't paying the £25 they charged to see Manchester United the next evening. Instead, the following day, ten of us defied the ageing process by playing a five-a-side football game in Fairview Park.

Our star was James "Sniffer" Lundon from Limerick, who put at least five past the opposing defence. Gavin "Cantona" Burnage from Yorkshire was in top form as our midfield dynamo. His Cantonesque facial features are such that the Leeds hordes who packed the Cat & Cage bar before the Leeds v Shelbourne game (this is true, I am not making it up) collectively pointed at him and chanted "you are Eric Cantona, you are Eric Cantona ..."

My own performance, which purists might describe in technical footballing terms as "crap", was somewhat mitigated by a successful assist to Sniffer Lundon, an early run-in with the ground from which my knee has yet to recover, a nice black eye (thank you, John Lowe), and the fact that several of my vital organs are reminding me that a decade is marginally too long to leave between your last football game and your next one.

The following day I nursed my knee injury through an evening out with another group of friends. We discussed the meaning of life, computers and the universe in general over a pleasant meal in the excellent Poco Loco restaurant in Parliament Street. The evening ended with ambitious plans being made for a Sunday go-karting session in Santry.

So what's all this doing in a book about the Internet? Well, I first met all the people involved through the Internet. The football crowd are subscribers to the Leeds United and League of Ireland football mailing lists, and the others members of the Internet Eireann (an Internet Access Provider) Users Group. And they say that the Internet is a depersonalising force in society ...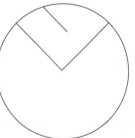

The URL File	**The Gallup Organisation — http://www.gallup.com/**

Online chat and online games

← B7
Socialising
on the
Internet

There are three areas of online socialising that are used less
frequently than mailing lists and newsgroups. You may well be
very interested in these areas, but you are unlikely to start off
using them the first day you go online. So, whenever, you reach
the stage of wanting to find out more about them, go to the
following addresses on the World Wide Web...

IRC, MUDs, PBM and other SOIs (sets of initials)

IRC (Internet Relay Chat)
The CB radio of the Internet. For details on what it is, how to
get started, technichal info, channels and people and other
IRC World Wide Web links, go to the Web page at
http://http1.brunel.ac.uk:8080/~cs93jtl/IRC.html
or to any IRC references at *http://www.yahoo.com/*

MUDs (Multi-User Dungeons)
Text-based fantasy games in which you play the part of a
character by typing in the decisions he or she makes as the
game progresses. (also known as Multi-user Dimensions or
Domains.) For further info, go to the Web page at
http://draco.centerline.com:8080/~franl/mud.html
or to any MUD references at *http://www.yahoo.com/*

PBM (Play By Mail)
A large variety of games can be played by either postal mail
or electronic mail. The Usenet newsgroup *rec.games.pbm*
discusses these. For further info, go to the Web page at
http://fermi.clas.virginia.edu/~gl8f/pbm.html
or to any PBM references at *http://www.yahoo.com/*

Mailing lists and newsgroups

When you start out on the Internet, your first stop for socialising
is likely to be either a mailing list or a newsgroup. There are
thousands of options available, and you will certainly find one or
more to match your specific interests. The following pages include
a sample A–Z of mailing lists and some of the thousands of
newsgroups you can subscribe to.

The Games Domain — http://wcl-rs.bham.ac.uk/GamesDomain	The URL File

A sample A–Z of social and fun mailing lists

ARCH-L
Archaeology List, Subscribers: 1500+
List address: *arch-l@tamvm1.tamu.edu*
You can join this list by sending the message
"sub ARCH-L your name" to *listserv@tamvm1.tamu.edu*

BBSHOP
For Those Interested in Barbershop Harmony, Subscribers: 950+
List address: *bbshop@admin.humberc.on.ca*
You can join this list by sending the message
"sub BBSHOP your name" to *listserv@admin.humberc.on.ca*

CLAYART
Ceramic Arts Discussion List, Subscribers: 1350+
List address: *clayart@ukcc.uky.edu*
You can join this list by sending the message
"sub CLAYART your name" to *listserv@ukcc.uky.edu*

DQMW-L
Dr Quinn Medicine Woman TV Show, Subscribers: 370+
List address: *dqmw-l@emuvm1.cc.emory.edu*
You can join this list by sending the message
"sub DQMW-L your name" to *listserv@emuvm1.cc.emory.edu*

ERNEST
Discussion of Ernest Hemingway and his works, Subscribers: 40+, List address: *ernest@cfrvm.cfr.usf.edu*
You can join this list by sending the message
"sub ERNEST your name" to *listserv@cfrvm.cfr.usf.edu*

FEMJUR
Discussions and Information About Feminist Legal Issues
Subscribers: 700+
List address: *femjur@listserv.syr.edu*
You can join this list by sending the message
"sub FEMJUR your name" to *listserv@listserv.syr.edu*

GARDENS
Gardens & Gardening, Subscribers: 1500+
List address: *gardens@ukcc.uky.edu*
You can join this list by sending the message
"sub GARDENS your name" to *listserv@ukcc.uky.edu*

← B7
Socialising on the Internet

← B2
Subscribing to a mailing list

→ D2
Group discussion netiquette

These pages contain a small sample of the many fun and social topics that have their own discussion mailing lists. You can get a full list of mailing lists at the World Wide Web address *http://www. tile.net/*

A sample A–Z of social and fun mailing lists

HOUNDS-L
Discussion of Sherlock Holmes Literature, Subscribers: 370+
List address: *hounds-l@kentvm.kent.edu*
You can join this list by sending the message
"sub HOUNDS-L your name" to *listserv@kentvm.kent.edu*

INTER-EU
A discussion list for International Educators in Europe and
beyond, Subscribers: 240+
List address: *inter-eu@nic.surfnet.nl*
You can join this list by sending the message
"sub INTER-EU your name" to *listserv@nic.surfnet.nl*

JAZZ-L
Jazz Lovers' List, Subscribers: 370+
List address: *jazz-l@brownvm.brown.edu*
You can join this list by sending the message
"sub JAZZ-L your name" to *listserv@brownvm.brown.edu*

KIDCAFE
KIDCAFE Youth Dialog, Subscribers: 1300+
List address: *kidcafe@vm1.nodak.edu*
You can join this list by sending the message
"sub KIDCAFE your name" to *listserv@vm1.nodak.edu*

LDRSHP
Discussion about all aspects of leadership, Subscribers: 450+
List address: *ldrshp@iubvm.ucs.indiana.edu*
You can join this list by sending the message
"sub LDRSHP your name" to *listserv@iubvm.ucs.indiana.edu*

MMEDIA-L
Multimedia discussion list, Subscribers: 670+
List address: *mmedia-l@itesmvf1.rzs.itesm.mx*
You can join this group by sending the message
"sub MMEDIA-L your name" to *listserv@itesmvf1.rzs.itesm.mx*

NEW-LIST
New List Announcements (University College Dublin, Ireland)
Subscribers: 700+
List address: *new-list@irlearn.ucd.ie*
You can join this list by sending the message
"sub NEW-LIST your name" to *listserv@irlearn.ucd.ie*

← B7
Socialising
on the
Internet

← B2
Subscribing
to a mailing
list

→ D2
Group
discussion
netiquette

These pages
contain a
small sample
of the many
fun and
social topics
that have
their own
discussion
mailing lists.
You can get
a full list of
mailing lists
at the World
Wide Web
address
*http://www.
tile.net/*

Glasgow Celtic — http://ugwww.ucs.ed.ac.uk/~tony/celtic.html   The URL File

A sample A–Z of social and fun mailing lists

← B7
Socialising on the Internet

← B2
Subscribing to a mailing list

→ D2
Group discussion netiquette

OCD-L
Obsessive Compulsive Disorder List, Subscribers: 270+
List address: *ocd-l@vm.marist.edu*
You can join this list by sending the message
"sub OCD-L your name" to *listserv@vm.marist.edu*

PETBUNNY
Forum for folks with companion rabbits, Subscribers: 270+
List address: *petbunny@ukcc.uky.edu*
You can join this list by sending the message
"sub PETBUNNY your name" to *listserv@ukcc.uky.edu*

QUAKER-L
Quaker concerns re community & spirituality, Subscribers: 530+
List address: *quaker-l@vmd.cso.uiuc.edu*
You can join this list by sending the message
"sub QUAKER-L your name" to *listserv@vmd.cso.uiuc.edu*

RUSHTALK
Open discussion of current US events (Rush Limbaugh style)
Subscribers: 130+
List address: *rushtalk@athena.csdco.com*
You can join this list by sending the message
"sub RUSHTALK your name" to *listserv@athena.csdco.com*

SCUBA-L
Scuba diving discussion list, Subscribers: 550+
List address: *scuba-l@brownvm.brown.edu*
You can join this list by sending the message
"sub SCUBA-L your name" to *listserv@brownvm.brown.edu*

TFTD-L
Thought For The Day, Subscribers: 4000+
List address: *tftd-l@tamvm1.tamu.edu*
You can join this group by sending the message
"sub TFTD-L your name" to *listserv@tamvm1.tamu.edu*

UWSA
United We Stand America (Ross Perot support group)
Subscribers: 70+
List address: *uwsa@miamiu.muohio.edu*
You can join this list by sending the message
"sub UWSA your name" to *listserv@miamiu.muohio.edu*

These pages contain a small sample of the many fun and social topics that have their own discussion mailing lists. You can get a full list of mailing lists at the World Wide Web address *http://www. tile.net/*

A sample A–Z of social and fun mailing lists

VRINST-L
Virtual Reality - Implications for Instruction, Subscribers: 30+
List address: *vrinst-l@uwf.cc.uwf.edu*
You can join this list by sending the message
"sub VRINST-L your name" to *listserv@uwf.cc.uwf.edu*

WRITING
Fiction Writers Workshop Discussion List, Subscribers: 450+
List address: *writing@psuvm.psu.edu*
You can join this group by sending the message
"sub WRITING your name" to *listserv@psuvm.psu.edu*

XLFORT-L
XL FORTRAN Compilers Discussion List, Subscribers: 4
List address: *xlfort-l@uga.cc.uga.edu*
You can join this list by sending the message
"sub XLFORT-L your name" to *listserv@uga.cc.uga.edu*

Y-RIGHTS
Y-Rights: Kid/Teen Rights Discussion Group
Subscribers: 230+
List address: *y-rights@sjuvm.stjohns.edu*
You can join this list by sending the message
"sub Y-RIGHTS your name" to *listserv@sjuvm.stjohns.edu*

ZAPP
Zapp! The Lightning of Empowerment
Subscribers: 170+
List address: *zapp@ucsfvm.ucsf.edu*
You can join this list by sending the message
"sub ZAPP your name" to *listserv@ucsfvm.ucsf.edu*

← B7
Socialising on the Internet

← B2
Subscribing to a mailing list

→ D2
Group discussion netiquette

These pages contain a small sample of the many fun and social topics that have their own discussion mailing lists. You can get a full list of mailing lists at the World Wide Web address *http://www.tile.net/*

The 5 Absolutely Best Mailing Lists Ever

Well, okay then, the five mailing lists that are my **favourites** of the ones that I have subscribed to since I started on the Net — along with my favourite newsgroups and Web pages. As you might expect, they mainly reflect my personal interests but they also regularly include very interesting information and contributions.

→ D7

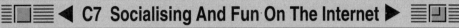
A small sample of social and fun newsgroups ...

← B7
Socialising on the Internet

← B2
Subscribing to a Usenet newsgroup

→ D2
Group discussion netiquette

alt.books.arthur-clarke,	alt.drugs,
alt.books.isaac-asimov,	alt.drugs.caffeine,
alt.books.reviews,	alt.drugs.psychedelics,
alt.books.stephen-king,	alt.drunken.bastards,
alt.books.toffler,	alt.drwho.creative,
alt.books.tom-clancy,	alt.elvis.king,
alt.buddha.short.fat.guy,	alt.elvis.sighting,
alt.california,	alt.fan.actors,
alt.callahans,	alt.fan.addams.family,
alt.celebrities,	alt.fan.barry-manilow,
alt.coffee,	alt.fan.bill-gates,
alt.collecting.autographs,	alt.fan.blues-brothers,
alt.collecting.teddy-bears,	alt.fan.brian-ellis,
alt.comedy.british,	alt.fan.brie,
alt.comedy.british.blackadder,	alt.fan.british-accent,
alt.comedy.slapstick,	alt.fan.courtney-love,
alt.comedy.standup,	alt.fan.dan-quayle,
alt.comedy.vaudeville,	alt.fan.dave_barry,
alt.comics.alternative,	alt.fan.david-bowie,
alt.comics.batman,	alt.fan.douglas-adams,
alt.comics.superman,	alt.fan.elvis-costello,
alt.consciousness,	alt.fan.frank-zappa,
alt.consciousness.mysticism,	alt.fan.g-gordon-liddy,
alt.conspiracy,	alt.fan.goons,
alt.conspiracy.jfk,	alt.fan.howard-stern,
alt.consumers.free-stuff,	alt.fan.itchy-n-scratchy,
alt.cooking-chat,	alt.fan.james-bond,
alt.creative-cook,	alt.fan.jay-leno,
alt.creative-cooking,	alt.fan.jesus-christ,
alt.cuddle,	alt.fan.kate-moss,
alt.cult-movies,	alt.fan.kathy-jo,
alt.cult-movies.rocky-horror	alt.fan.laurie.anderson,
alt.divination,	alt.fan.letterman,
alt.dreams,	alt.fan.lightbulbs,
alt.dreams.lucid,	alt.fan.lion-king,
alt.drinks.kool-aid,	alt.fan.madonna,

These pages contain a small sample of the many fun and social topics covered by the Usenet newsgroups. There are thousands more groups than those listed here and new groups are created every day.

... a small sample of social and fun newsgroups ...

alt.fan.mel-brooks,
alt.fan.mike-chapman,
alt.fan.monty-python,
alt.fan.penn-n-teller,
alt.fan.pratchett,
alt.fan.ren-and-stimpy,
alt.fan.rickie-lee-jones,
alt.fan.ronald-reagan,
alt.fan.rush-limbaugh,
alt.fan.schwarzenegger,
alt.fan.spinal-tap,
alt.fan.sting,
alt.fan.tanya-harding,
alt.fan.tarantino,
alt.fan.teen.idols,
alt.fan.tolkien,
alt.fan.tom-clancy,
alt.fan.tom-robbins,
alt.fan.u2,
alt.fan.vic-reeves,
alt.fan.weird-al,
alt.fan.winona-ryder,
alt.fan.wodehouse,
alt.fan.woody-allen,
alt.fashion,
alt.feminazis,
alt.feminism,
alt.fishing,
alt.flame,
alt.folklore.college,
alt.folklore.computers,
alt.folklore.ghost-stories,
alt.folklore.herbs,
alt.folklore.info,
alt.folklore.internet,
alt.folklore.military,

alt.folklore.science,
alt.folklore.suburban,
alt.folklore.urban,
alt.food,
alt.food.cocacola,
alt.food.coffee,
alt.food.dennys,
alt.food.fat-free,
alt.food.ice-cream,
alt.food.mcdonalds,
alt.food.pancakes,
alt.food.red-lobster,
alt.food.sushi,
alt.food.waffle-house,
alt.food.wine,
alt.forgery,
alt.freaks,
alt.freedom.of.information.act,
alt.gambling,
alt.games.doom,
alt.games.video.classic,
alt.geek,
alt.genealogy,
alt.good.morning,
alt.good.news,
alt.gothic,
alt.graffiti,
alt.guitar,
alt.guitar.bass,
alt.health.oxygen-therapy,
alt.hindu,
alt.history.living,
alt.history.what-if,
alt.home.repair,
alt.homosexual,
alt.horror,

← B7
Socialising
on the
Internet

← B2
Subscribing
to a Usenet
newsgroup

→ D2
Group
discussion
netiquette

These pages
contain a
small sample
of the many
fun and
social topics
covered by
the Usenet
newsgroups.
There are
thousands
more groups
than those
listed here
and new
groups are
created
every day.

... a small sample of social and fun newsgroups ...

← B7
Socialising on the Internet

← B2
Subscribing to a Usenet newsgroup

→ D2
Group discussion netiquette

alt.horror.werewolves,
alt.hotrod,
alt.human-brain,
alt.humor.best-of-usenet,
alt.humor.oracle,
alt.humor.puns,
alt.hypnosis,
alt.illuminati,
alt.impeach.clinton,
alt.individualism,
alt.internet.talk.bizarre,
alt.irc.announce,
alt.irc.questions,
alt.irc.recovery,
alt.jokes.limericks,
alt.journalism,
alt.kill.the.whales,
alt.law-enforcement,
alt.lefthanders,
alt.lemmings,
alt.lies,
alt.life.afterlife,
alt.magic.secrets,
alt.make.money.fast,
alt.marketplace.funky-stuff.forsale,
alt.masonic.members,
alt.mcdonalds,
alt.meditation,
alt.mindcontrol,
alt.models,
alt.motorcycles.harley,
alt.msdos.programmer,
alt.msn.sucks,
alt.music.4-track,
alt.music.alternative,

alt.music.alternative.female,
alt.music.amy-grant,
alt.music.beastie-boys,
alt.music.billy-joel,
alt.music.bjork,
alt.music.bootlegs,
alt.music.brian-eno,
alt.music.deep-purple,
alt.music.depeche-mode,
alt.music.enya,
alt.music.erasure,
alt.music.fleetwood-mac,
alt.music.genesis,
alt.music.independent,
alt.music.info-society,
alt.music.j-s-bach,
alt.music.james-taylor,
alt.music.jethro-tull,
alt.music.jimi.hendrix,
alt.music.karaoke,
alt.music.kylie-minogue,
alt.music.led-zeppelin,
alt.music.les-moore,
alt.music.live,
alt.music.lloyd-webber,
alt.music.misc,
alt.music.monkees,
alt.music.moody-blues,
alt.music.nirvana,
alt.music.paul-simon,
alt.music.pearl-jam,
alt.music.pet-shop-boys,
alt.music.peter-gabriel,
alt.music.pink-floyd,
alt.music.prince,
alt.music.progressive,

These pages contain a small sample of the many fun and social topics covered by the Usenet newsgroups. There are thousands more groups than those listed here and new groups are created every day.

... a small sample of social and fun newsgroups ...

alt.music.queen,
alt.music.ska,
alt.music.squeeze,
alt.music.swedish-pop,
alt.music.the-doors,
alt.music.the.police,
alt.music.u2,
alt.music.weird-al,
alt.music.who,
alt.my.head.hurts,
alt.mythology,
alt.net.scandal,
alt.newbie,
alt.newbies,
alt.news-media,
alt.nosebeeping,
alt.nuke.the.USA,
alt.org.earth-first,
alt.org.food-not-bombs,
alt.out-of-body,
alt.overlords,
alt.pagan,
alt.pantyhose,
alt.parallel.universes,
alt.paranormal,
alt.party,
alt.pave.the.earth,
alt.personals,
alt.personals.fetish,
alt.pets.rabbits,
alt.philosophy.zen,
alt.politics.british,
alt.politics.clinton,
alt.politics.correct,
alt.politics.ec,
alt.politics.economics,

alt.politics.elections,
alt.politics.europe.misc,
alt.politics.greens,
alt.politics.org.covert,
alt.politics.perot,
alt.politics.radical-left,
alt.postmodern,
alt.privacy,
alt.prophecies.nostradamus,
alt.prose,
alt.psychology,
alt.punk,
alt.radio.pirate,
alt.recovery,
alt.religion.all-worlds,
alt.religion.buddhism.tibetan,
alt.religion.christian,
alt.religion.islam,
alt.religion.scientology,
alt.religion.universal-life,
alt.revenge,
alt.revisionism,
alt.revolution.counter,
alt.rock-n-roll,
alt.rock-n-roll.acdc,
alt.rock-n-roll.aerosmith,
alt.rock-n-roll.metal.heavy,
alt.rock-n-roll.oldies,
alt.rock-n-roll.stones,
alt.romance,
alt.romance.chat,
alt.satellite.tv.europe,
alt.save.the.earth,
alt.school.homework-help,
alt.scooter,
alt.self-improve,

← B7
Socialising on the Internet

← B2
Subscribing to a Usenet newsgroup

→ D2
Group discussion netiquette

These pages contain a small sample of the many fun and social topics covered by the Usenet newsgroups. There are thousands more groups than those listed here and new groups are created every day.

... a small sample of social and fun newsgroups ...

alt.sewing,
alt.sex,
alt.sex.boredom,
alt.sex.exhibitionism,
alt.sex.fetish.tickling,
alt.sex.movies,
alt.sex.spanking,
alt.sex.stories,
alt.sex.woody-allen,
alt.shenanigans,
alt.silly.group.names.d,
alt.skate,
alt.skate-board,
alt.smokers,
alt.smokers.pipes,
alt.society.civil-liberties,
alt.society.generation-x,
alt.society.kindness,
alt.sport.bowling,
alt.sport.bungee,
alt.sport.darts,
alt.sport.paintball,
alt.sport.racquetball,
alt.sport.squash,
alt.stagecraft,
alt.startrek.klingon,
alt.startrek.vulcan,
alt.stupidity,
alt.suburbs,
alt.support,
alt.support.depression,
alt.support.diet,
alt.support.dissociation,
alt.support.shyness,
alt.surfing,
alt.surrealism,

alt.sustainable.agriculture,
alt.swedish.chef.bork.bork.bork,
alt.tasteless,
alt.tasteless.jokes,
alt.travel.road-trip,
alt.true-crime,
alt.tv.animaniacs,
alt.tv.babylon-5,
alt.tv.beavis-n-butthead,
alt.tv.brady-bunch,
alt.tv.brisco-county,
alt.tv.commercials,
alt.tv.game-shows,
alt.tv.kungfu,
alt.tv.man-from-uncle,
alt.tv.mash,
alt.tv.muppets,
alt.tv.prisoner,
alt.tv.red-dwarf,
alt.tv.rockford-files,
alt.tv.roseanne,
alt.tv.simpsons,
alt.tv.star-trek.ds9,
alt.tv.x-files,
alt.video.laserdisc,
alt.wedding,
alt.white_house.invasion,
alt.zines,
misc.activism.progressive,
misc.books.technical,
misc.consumers,
misc.creativity,
misc.education,
misc.entrepreneurs,
misc.fitness,
misc.fitness.aerobic,

← B7
Socialising on the Internet

← B2
Subscribing to a Usenet newsgroup

→ D2
Group discussion netiquette

These pages contain a small sample of the many fun and social topics covered by the Usenet newsgroups. There are thousands more groups than those listed here and new groups are created every day.

... a small sample of social and fun newsgroups ...

misc.forsale.computers,
misc.health.alternative,
misc.invest,
misc.kids,
misc.kids.pregnancy,
misc.kids.vacation,
misc.misc,
misc.transport.urban-transit,
misc.wanted,
misc.writing,
misc.writing.screenplays,
rec.antiques,
rec.aquaria,
rec.arts.animation,
rec.arts.books,
rec.arts.books.childrens,
rec.arts.books.reviews,
rec.arts.cinema,
rec.arts.comics.strips,
rec.arts.dance,
rec.arts.disney,
rec.arts.drwho,
rec.arts.erotica,
rec.arts.fine,
rec.arts.int-fiction,
rec.arts.manga,
rec.arts.movies.reviews,
rec.arts.poems,
rec.arts.prose,
rec.arts.startrek.info,
rec.arts.startrek.misc,
rec.arts.startrek.reviews,
rec.arts.theatre,
rec.arts.theatre.musicals,
rec.arts.theatre.plays,
rec.arts.theatre.stagecraft,

rec.arts.tv.uk,
rec.arts.tv.uk.comedy,
rec.arts.tv.uk.coronation-st,
rec.arts.tv.uk.eastenders,
rec.arts.tv.uk.misc,
rec.audio.misc,
rec.autos.antique,
rec.aviation.piloting,
rec.bicycles.racing,
rec.birds,
rec.boats,
rec.climbing,
rec.collecting,
rec.collecting.coins,
rec.collecting.dolls,
rec.collecting.phonecards,
rec.collecting.stamps,
rec.crafts.brewing,
rec.crafts.jewelry,
rec.crafts.quilting,
rec.crafts.winemaking,
rec.drugs.cannabis,
rec.folk-dancing,
rec.food.cooking,
rec.food.drink,
rec.food.drink.beer,
rec.food.drink.coffee,
rec.food.recipes,
rec.food.restaurants,
rec.food.veg.cooking,
rec.gambling,
rec.gambling.misc,
rec.games.board,
rec.games.chess,
rec.games.design,
rec.games.diplomacy,

← B7
Socialising on the Internet

← B2
Subscribing to a Usenet newsgroup

→ D2
Group discussion netiquette

These pages contain a small sample of the many fun and social topics covered by the Usenet newsgroups. There are thousands more groups than those listed here and new groups are created every day.

... a small sample of social and fun newsgroups ...

rec.games.miniatures,
rec.games.pinball,
rec.games.video.arcade,
rec.gardens,
rec.gardens.orchids,
rec.gardens.roses,
rec.guns,
rec.heraldry,
rec.humor,
rec.humor.funny,
rec.humor.oracle,
rec.humour,
rec.hunting,
rec.juggling,
rec.kites,
rec.martial-arts,
rec.models.railroad,
rec.motorcycles,
rec.music.beatles,
rec.music.celtic,
rec.music.christian,
rec.music.classical,
rec.music.compose,
rec.music.country.western,
rec.music.dylan,
rec.music.early,
rec.music.folk,
rec.music.funky,
rec.music.makers.guitar,
rec.music.movies,
rec.org.mensa,
rec.outdoors.fishing,
rec.photo.advanced,
rec.photo.darkroom,
rec.photo.help,
rec.puzzles,

rec.puzzles.crosswords,
rec.radio.amateur.misc,
rec.roller-coaster,
rec.running,
rec.scouting,
rec.scuba,
rec.skate,
rec.skiing.alpine,
rec.skydiving,
rec.sport.archery,
rec.sport.baseball,
rec.sport.basketball.europe,
rec.sport.billiard,
rec.sport.boxing,
rec.sport.cricket,
rec.sport.disc,
rec.sport.fencing,
rec.sport.football.pro,
rec.sport.golf,
rec.sport.hockey,
rec.sport.hockey.field,
rec.sport.misc,
rec.sport.olympics,
rec.sport.paintball,
rec.sport.pro-wrestling,
rec.sport.rowing,
rec.sport.rugby,
rec.sport.soccer,
rec.sport.swimming,
rec.sport.table-tennis,
rec.sport.tennis,
rec.sport.triathlon,
rec.sport.unicycling,
rec.sport.volleyball,
rec.sport.water-polo,
rec.sport.waterski,

← B7
Socialising on the Internet

← B2
Subscribing to a Usenet newsgroup

→ D2
Group discussion netiquette

These pages contain a small sample of the many fun and social topics covered by the Usenet newsgroups. There are thousands more groups than those listed here and new groups are created every day.

... a small sample of social and fun newsgroups

rec.toys.lego,
rec.toys.misc,
rec.travel,
rec.travel.air,
rec.travel.cruises,
rec.travel.europe,
rec.travel.marketplace,
rec.travel.misc,
rec.travel.usa-canada,
rec.video,
rec.video.production,
rec.video.releases,
rec.windsurfing,
rec.woodworking,
soc.answers,
soc.couples,
soc.culture.australian,
soc.culture.brazil,
soc.culture.british,
soc.culture.celtic,
soc.culture.europe,
soc.culture.irish,
soc.culture.south-africa,
soc.culture.usa,
soc.culture.yugoslavia,
soc.feminism,
soc.genealogy.misc,
soc.genealogy.surnames,
soc.genealogy.uk+ireland,
soc.history,
soc.history.war.misc,
soc.history.war.world-war-ii,
soc.history.what-if,
soc.libraries.talk,
soc.men,
soc.motss,

soc.net-people,
soc.org.nonprofit,
soc.penpals,
soc.politics,
soc.religion.bahai,
soc.religion.christian,
soc.religion.eastern,
soc.religion.islam,
soc.religion.unitarian-univ,
soc.rights.human,
soc.roots,
soc.singles,
soc.veterans,
soc.women,
talk.abortion,
talk.answers,
talk.bizarre,
talk.environment,
talk.euthanasia,
talk.origins,
talk.philosophy.misc,
talk.politics.animals,
talk.politics.crypto,
talk.politics.drugs,
talk.politics.european-union,
talk.politics.guns,
talk.politics.libertarian,
talk.politics.medicine,
talk.politics.mideast,
talk.politics.misc,
talk.politics.soviet,
talk.politics.theory,
talk.politics.tibet, talk.rape,
talk.religion.misc,
talk.religion.newage,
talk.rumors

← B7
Socialising on the Internet

← B2
Subscribing to a Usenet newsgroup

→ D2
Group discussion netiquette

These pages contain a small sample of the many fun and social topics covered by the Usenet newsgroups. There are thousands more groups than those listed here and new groups are created every day.

A sample A–Z of social and fun Web sites...

← **B8**
Surfing the World Wide Web

→ **C13**
Irish Web Page Directory

Athletics
The Official Information Services of the 1995 5th IAAF World Championships in Athletics; includes results, statistics and records of all events and profiles and records of all of the athletes who competed.
http://www.wca95.org/thechamp/

Books
An index of hundreds of on-line books. It also points to some common repositories of on-line books and other documents. Includes more than 850 English works.
http://www.cs.cmu.edu/Web/books.html

Cartoon Laws
The Top 83 Laws of Cartoons, including
Everything falls faster than an anvil, and
It's always either duck season or rabbit season.
http://www.dtd.com/keepers/keepers.cgi?toplist+8/12/1995

Dessert Recipes
Hundreds of dessert recipes including cakes, ice creams, pancakes, puddings, sweet souffles and sweet pies.
http://www.vuw.ac.nz/who/Amy.Gale/recipes/dessert/dessert.html

Eddie Izzard
"I don't wear women's clothes, they're my own"
Biography, interview, tour dates, reviews, readers comments.
http://www.xs4all.nl/~vonb/iz/izzard.html

Fawlty Towers
"Batteries, eh? Do you know something? You disgust me! I know what people like you get up to, and I think it's _disgusting_." An episode guide with topics and casts for both series, along with links to bits from the scripts.
http://www.cm.cf.ac.uk/Fun/FawltyTowers.html

Genres of Music
Hundreds of pages on A Cappella, Ambient, Bluegrass, Blues,

These pages contain a small A–Z sample of the many thousands of Web sites from which you can start a surfing session. As the Web is constantly changing, some of these pages may have moved or expired. Don't be intimidated by the long addresses, you only have to type them in once and you can then save them in your browser's bookmark file.

The URL File	I Ching — http://cad.ucla.edu/8001/iching

A sample A–Z of social and fun Web sites...

← B8
Surfing the World Wide Web

→ C13
Irish Web Page Directory

Cajun, Classical, C&W, Disco, Ethnic, Flamenco, Folk, Gothic, Instrumental, Jazz, New Age, Oldies, Polka, Progressive, Punk, Ska, Rap, Hip Hop, Reggae, Rock & Roll, Samba...
http://www.yahoo.com/Entertainment/Music/Genres/

Heather Has Two Mommies...
A children's story sponsored by the Massachusetts Institute of Appropriate Inclusivity (formerly "Political Correctness" until that term was co-opted by the white power elite as a tool for attacking multiculturalism).
http://www-swiss.ai.mit.edu/zoo/heather-has-two-mommies.html

Ireland — The Virtual Tourist Guide
Categories include the four provinces, Irish universities, tracing your Irish ancestors, the Irish language, Irish literature, theatre, music, economics, politics and current affairs.
http://www.bess.tcd.ie/ireland.htm

Jokes About Economists
Q: Why did God create economists?
A: In order to make weather forecasters look good.
As the title suggests, a page of jokes about economists.
http://www.etla.fi/pkm/joke.html

Kids and Parents
Links for the whole family. Includes (for children) online fairytales, Mindlink magazine, knowbase for teenagers, a global show and tell; and (for parents) focus on the family, parent info network, fathers' forum and parenting resource centre.
http://pages.prodigy.com/ID/merit/meritkids.html

Literature
Authors whose works appear on the Web, including Austen, Byron, Coleridge, Defoe, Dickinson, Doyle, Erasmus, Joyce, Keats, Poe, Shelley, Shakespeare, Tolkien and Wordsworth.
http://www.cloud9.net/~scharf/writers.html

Monty Python
Yahoo's set of links to Monty Python pages on the Web,

URLs — Web page addresses, like FTP site addresses, are called URLs, which stands for Uniform Resource Locator (or Universal Resource Locator — there's no uniform agreement as to which it is).

A URL should be typed in exactly as it appears, with upper and lower case letters as they appear in the URL.

Intel — http://www.intel.com

The URL File

A sample A–Z of social and fun Web sites...

← B8
Surfing
the World
Wide Web

→ C13
Irish Web
Page
Directory

including the Holy Home Page of Antioch and a complete compilation of all Python scripts.
http://www.yahoo.com/Entertainment/Movies_and_Films/Titles/ Monty_Python/

Names Which Sound Like Or Are Verbs
Possibly the least useful page on the Internet, which is quite an achievement. Allows an alphabetical search of people's first names that sound like verbs (such as Carrie, Doug, Flo or Vito) or that actually are verbs (such as Lance, Pat, Rob or Rush)
http://fas-www.harvard.edu/~jsbloom/name_verb.html

Olympic Games 1996
Everything you need to know about the 1996 Olympic Games in Atlanta, including updates on the sports and venues, the official programme, travel and ticket information, sponsors etc.
http://www.atlanta.olympic.org/

Propaganda Analysis
Very interesting analysis of common propaganda techniques such as word games, false connections, special appeals, logical fallacies, and unwarranted extrapolations.
http://carmen.artsci.washington.edu/propaganda/home.htm

Quotations
A quote a day, updated weekly with seven new quotes and a bonus quote for free. "Sometimes one pays most for the things one gets for nothing." — Albert Einstein.
http://pubweb.ucdavis.edu/Documents/Quotations/wq-index.html

Recyler's World
A very comprehensive resource centre for information relating to secondary or recyclable commodities, by-products, used and surplus items or materials and collectible items.
http://granite.sentex.net/recycle/

Soccer
A comprehensive list of all the football-related Web pages in the world. Includes links to pages about Irish, British and

These pages contain a small A–Z sample of the many thousands of Web sites from which you can start a surfing session. As the Web is constantly changing, some of these pages may have moved or expired. Don't be intimidated by the long addresses, you only have to type them in once and you can then save them in your browser's bookmark file.

The URL File | **Internet Information from InterNIC — http://www.internic.net**

A sample A–Z of social and fun Web sites...

← B8
Surfing the World Wide Web

→C13
Irish Web Page Directory

international club and national football homepages.
http://www.atm.ch.cam.ac.uk/sports/webs.html

Theology
Links to serious Christian theological activity on the Internet.
http://apu.edu/~bstone/theology.html

Useless Page
The original useless page with links to some of the absolute worst of the Net.
http://www.primus.com/staff/paulp/useless.html

Veggies Unite!
A searchable vegetarian cookbook, includes recipes by category or alphabetically, a listing of veg-minded events around the world, plus info on health, medicine and nutrition.
http://www.honors.indiana.edu/~veggie/recipes.cgi/

Weekly Web News
Tabloid Journalism on the Web — a spoof newsletter vis-à-vis the infamous American Weekly World News.
http://www.geopages.com/RodeoDrive/1044/

Xmas, Twelve Days Of
A politically correct version of the popular Christmas carol.
"On the 12th day of the Eurocentrically imposed midwinter festival, my potential-acquaintance-rape-survivor gave to me..."
http://www-swiss.ai.mit.edu/zoo/twelve-days.text

Youth
A guide to online resources for youth and youth workers, including links to Web pages, mailing lists and gophers.
http://www.ocsny.com/~mdm/guide.html

Zen FAQ (spoof version)
What is Zen? Why do Zen writings seem like nonsense? A spoof guide to Zen Buddhism. Also includes a link to the real Zen Buddhism FAQ (Frequently Asked Questions).
http://www.bga.com/~rlp/dwp/zen-faq.html

URLs — Web page addresses, like FTP site addresses, are called URLs, which stands for Uniform Resource Locator (or Universal Resource Locator — there's no uniform agreement as to which it is).

A URL should be typed in exactly as it appears, with upper and lower case letters as they appear in the URL.

'I think there is a world market for maybe five computers'

— *Chairman of IBM, 1943*

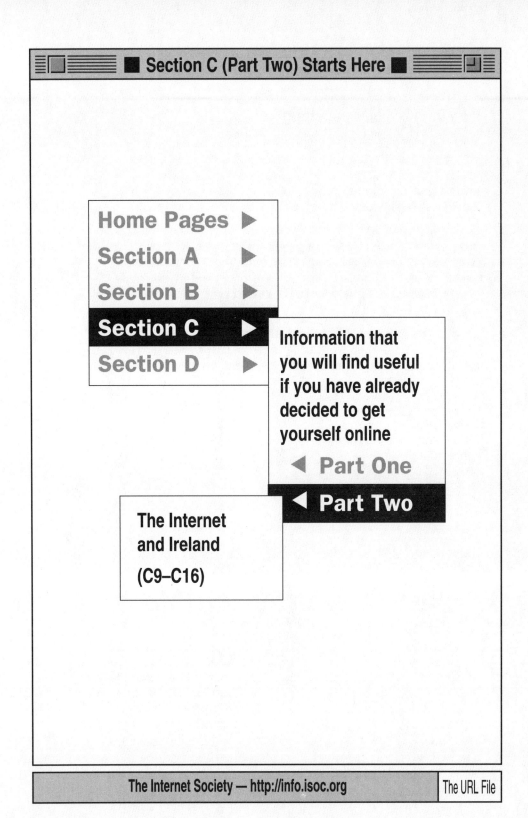

Home Pages ▶

Section A ▶

Section B ▶

Section C ▶

Section D ▶

Information that you will find useful if you have already decided to get yourself online

◀ **Part One**

◀ **Part Two**

The Internet and Ireland (C9–C16)

How long is a piece of string?

← B9
Who is the Internet?

How many people use the Internet? If you're a trainspotter type you might like to add this new statistic to your database of fascinating facts. If you're running a business and thinking of investing in an Internet presence, you need to know whether the figures being quoted to you are 100% accurate.

Sadly, you can't. Why? Three reasons. Firstly, the Internet is growing so fast that today's figures are out of date tomorrow. Secondly, while you can know how many host computers are linked to the Internet, it's impossible to accurately calculate how many people are using each of these computers.

Thirdly, "using the Internet" means different things to different people. The following is a conservative estimate of the number of people who in 1995 were using each of the various facilities that different people might describe as "using the Internet".

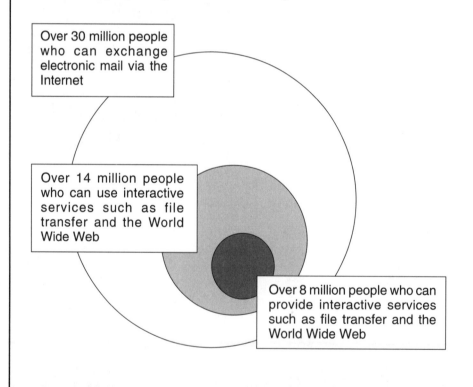

Over 30 million people who can exchange electronic mail via the Internet

Over 14 million people who can use interactive services such as file transfer and the World Wide Web

Over 8 million people who can provide interactive services such as file transfer and the World Wide Web

Double your money

← B9
Who is the Internet?

You may have heard the story about the man who was offered a month's work at either £50 a day or else 1p for the first day, 2p for the second day and, every day from then then on, double the amount that he had got on the previous day. If he took the £50 a day rate, he would end up with £1,550. If he took the penny doubling up each day, on the 31st day of the month he would get £10,737,418.24.

So figures repeatedly doubling add up to pretty impressive amounts very quickly. In July 1981 there were 213 computers on the Internet. If that figure had repeatedly doubled every year since then, there would have been over three and a half million computers on the net in July 1995. There were not. There were over six million.

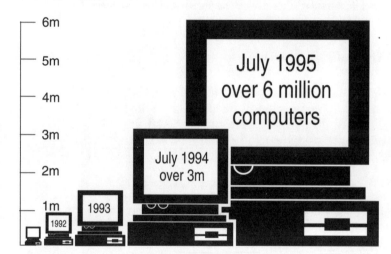

The Internet Society has projected the following estimate for growth in host computers between now and the year 2000:

July	1996	12,836,272	July	1998	46,967,385
Jan	1997	17,753,266	Jan	1999	64,958,464
July	1997	24,553,739	July	1999	89,841,111
Jan	1998	33,959,165	Jan	2000	124,255,175

A defence budget in need of a project

← B10
Who owns the Internet?

In the 1960s, the United States Department of Defence was funding the US space program under its Advanced Research Projects Agency (ARPA), run by the military. The space program was then transferred from military control to NASA, leaving ARPA with loads of money in its budget and nothing to spend it on.

Noticing that the Department of Defence had loads of computers, someone suggested that ARPA get involved in computer science research. A network of computers called the ARPANET was established, linking computers around America that were involved in ARPA research.

ARPAnet — the bomb-resistant network

In the late 1960s, the US Congress noticed that ARPA was spending defence budget money on non-military computer research. A quick slap on the wrist and a temporary name-change to the Defence Advanced Research Projects Agency (DARPA) followed.

The ARPANET itself, however, continued to be funded as it was deemed to be of military value. It linked computers together in a network where each computer knew where all of the others were, and could send information along the network even if one or more of the computers was not working.

As one of the reasons that one of the computers might not be working was that the pesky Russians might drop a large nuclear bomb on it (or so the US Defence Department feared), there were military attractions in the idea of a computer network that could work around such an inconvenience.

The URL File | **Jewish Global Network — http://www.mofet.macam98:ac.il/~dovw/t01.html**

A proliferation of networks

←B10
Who owns the Internet?

In the early 1980s the ARPANET was split into two networks, with ARPANET continuing with it's research communications, and Milnet (Military Network) carrying information between military sites. There was still some overlap, as some information went from one network to the other through interconnecting gateways.

Other networks such as Usenet (the Users' Network) and BITNET ("Because It's Time" Network) also started around the late 1970's and early 1980's. These were essentially co-operative networks, through which users tried to pass on information and software for as close as possible to free of charge. They are now both linked to the Internet through gateways.

NSFNET to the Information Superhighway

In 1986, the US National Science Foundation Network (NSFNET) was established to connect supercomputer sites throughout the USA. It also connected local and regional networks together. Its management was contracted to a group of three companies (IBM, MCI and Merit). It eventually took over from ARPANET to become the backbone of the Internet.

In recent years commercial involvement has started to reshape the Internet. It is now easier for an individual to get online, but as things evolve more services may have to be paid for by the end user. US Vice President Al Gore has popularised the idea of an Information Superhighway linking everything together at very high speeds. If this happens, the Internet will certainly be one of the major communications tools of the future.

John Peel's Playlists — http://www.bbcnc.org.uk/bbctv/radio1/j_peel | The URL File

TCP/IP and other letters of the alphabet

← B11
... if you
are a
computer

When you start asking around about the Internet, you may hear people talking about the TCP/IP suite. If you wish, you can just nod knowledgebly and say hmmm if under pressure to speak, and you will in all probability still manage to get successfully connected to the Internet. But if you are curious ... protocols are simply rules or conventions that a group of people or computers agree to be guided by. Computers linked to the Internet use the folowing protocols to communicate with each other:

IP (Internet Protocol)	This is a network protocol. What it does is route data from one host computer to another. IP does not guarantee that data will be delivered, just that it will do its best to deliver it to the IP address that it has been given.
TCP (Transmission Control Protocol) and UDP (User Datagram Protocol)	These are transport protocols. TCP collects related packets of information and makes sure that they are put back together again in the correct order when they arrive at their destination.
Application Protocols	These translate incoming information into a format that you can understand when using your computer. Each application (for mail, Web, file transfer etc.) has its own protocol.

The most common combination of protocols that is used by computers on the Internet is called the TCP/IP suite (or family). It includes TCP, IP and the protocols for the main applications used on the Internet. And you can happily use the Internet for a century without knowing the details of how they actually work.

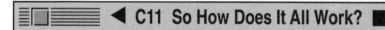 
Bandwidth and information transmission

← B11
... if you
are a
computer

Once you start using the Internet, another thing you will hear a lot about is bandwidth. The main purpose of bandwidth is that it provides an opportunity for people to complain that there is never enough of it. Bandwidth refers to the amount of data that can travel along a transmission line on the Internet. It is measured in bits per second, and refers to the capacity of the line, not the speed of the transmission. Think of it as the equivalent of water pipes: a wide water pipe can carry more water at any given time than a narrow one.

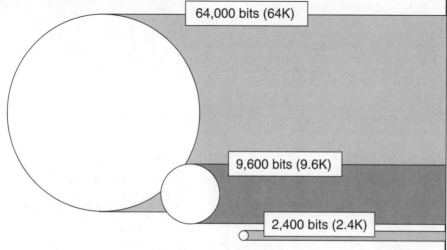

64,000 bits (64K)

9,600 bits (9.6K)

2,400 bits (2.4K)

How does bandwidth work in practice?

At the core of the Internet is a series of very high bandwidth lines, known as the backbone of the Internet. Linked to those lines are other lines of decreasing bandwidth, some of which are leased by Internet Service Providers. A Service Provider with, say, 64K or 128K of bandwidth then leases out access to that bandwidth to its subscribers. As not every subscriber will be using the line at the same time, Service Providers can lease out many times the actual bandwidth available to them. If that sounds like a licence to print money, it's because it may remind you of the principle that banks work on. However, bankers are rarely woken up to fix a system problem at 2 in the morning.

Juggling — http://www.hal.com/services/juggle/ | The URL File

2FM

Includes information on 2FM broadcasting frequencies for your area plus links to details of all the shows on 2FM —Breakfast Show With Ian Dempsey, Gerry Ryan Show, Larry Gogan with 2FM Jobsearch, Gareth O'Callaghan, Barry Lang, Hotline, Dave Fanning, Aidan Leonard, Mike Moloney, Weekend 2FM, Concerts, Roadcaster, Live Music, 2FM's Listener Top 10. 7Up Beat On The Streets.
http://ireland.iol.ie/resource/2fm/
Email: 2fm@iol.ie

2FM Music Artists Homepages

Very comprehensive set of links to home pages of musical artists including Eleanor McEvoy, Van Morrison, The Cranberries, Status Quo, Style Council, Boomtown Rats, Adam Ant, Ultravox, Elvis Costello, Sade, Phil Collins, Alison Moyet, Bryan Adams, U2, Beach Boys, Dire Straits, Sting, Queen, David Bowie, Simple Minds, The Pretenders, The Who, Santana, Elton John, Madonna, Paul McCartney, Alison Moyet, Eric Clapton, Duran Duran, Tina Turner, Bob Dylan ...
http://ireland.iol.ie/resource/2fm/artists.htm
Email: 2fm@iol.ie

Aardvark Guide to Cork

Includes information for visitors to Cork on exchange rates, travel, accommodation, places to eat, sightseeing, restaurants and pubs, plus planned links to details on local government, a calendar of events, a business directory and education facilities in Cork.
http://www.aardvark.ie/cork/
Email: admin@aardvark.ie

Aardvark Internet Publishing

A company which designs and maintains World Wide Web pages for companies, individuals and institutions. They also provide a professional design and consultancy service to companies who wish to set up and maintain their own internal World Wide Web server.

Links to pages created for clients including Beamish & Crawford, Cartoon Heaven (based in Melbourne, Australia) and Virtual Yachting, plus a guide to Cork City.
http://www.aardvark.ie/
Email: admin@aardvark.ie

Abbey & Peacock Theatres

What's showing at the Abbey and Peacock including reviews, performance times, booking information (you can reserve your choice of seats in seconds), an online diary of coming productions, and an introduction to the Abbey and its history.
http://www.internet-eireann.ie/
Adnet/clients/abbey/html/abbey.htm
Email: abbey@internet-eireann.ie.

Abbeyview Holiday Homes

Price list and services offered by Abbeyview holiday homes, situated within a five minute stroll of Kinsale town centre and close to two internationally recognised marinas, two golf courses plus tennis, swimming and horse-riding facilities.
http://www.internet-eireann.ie/Ireland/abbeyview.html

Accents Language Services

Home page of a Dublin based business which provides translations of texts, documents, films etc., plus interpreting, typesetting and printing in all European languages in any combination.
http://www.iol.ie/~accents/
Email: accents@iol.ie

Adnet

In business since 1994, Adnet provides marketing and technical skills to the Interactive Advertising market, for the small and medium-sized business or large corporation with complex requirements. Their Web pages include a business, arts, entertainment and shopping directory, plus links to pages created for their clients, including the Abbey and Peacock theatres, AMEV Insurance and the Irish American Partnership.
http://www.adnet.ie/Adnet/
Email: adnet@internet-eireann.ie

Aer Arann

Details of this company which has been flying

Note: As the Web is continually evolving, some of these pages may have moved or expired. Ask for details at the email address — if listed — which is less likely to have changed.

| The URL File | Justin's Underground Links — http://www.links.net |

for twenty five years, carrying islanders, tourists, scientists, film crews, cargo and even vital supplies to the Aran islands.
http://www.iol.ie/resource/aerarann/
Email: aerarann@iol.ie

Aer Lingus

A joint effort by Aer Lingus and IBM Ireland, this includes a comprehensive set of details on the airline's history, current fleet information, schedules and airport information, world-wide reservation numbers, service information, baggage allowances etc., Frequent Flyer Programme, Gold Circle Club, suggestions for short breaks and special offers.
http://www.hursley.ibm.com/aer/

AIB Group

The latest market news, analysis and information for the business user is available from a link to the AIB Corporate & Commercial Treasury page. The Daily Market Comment gives reports and rates, as well as a new feature topic each day. The Weekly Market Watch lists the key economic indicators and forecasts for this week. The Monthly Market Focus examines the ecomonic implications for the current month. AIB's guide to treasury risk management is also available on this page.
http://ireland.iol.ie/aib/
Email: aibtreas@iol.ie

Ain't Whistlin' Dixie

If you have a very fast Internet link and the right software, this page contains audio links to a collection of short samples of traditional music from Ireland, Scotland, England, Wales and America performed by David Walker on the Penny Whistle and Ocarina.
http://mothra.nts.uci.edu/~dhwalker/dixie/

Aisling Information Systems

An independent firm of information headed by Jim O'Reilly who has over 25 years experience in sourcing, handling, storing and retrieving information. Services offered include information brokerage, consultancy and auditing, the production of databases on CD-ROM, and the supply of text retrieval software packages.
http://www.ireland.net/marketplace/eirene/Aisling.html

All-Ireland Final 1995

4:58 pm: Vinnie Murphy is coming on for the last few moments for Dublin... 4:59 pm: Tyrone have just had a point disallowed for picking up the ball, well into injury time now, Dublin still lead by one point... 5:01 pm: The whistle has been blown!! Dublin have taken their 22nd All-Ireland final to the absolute delight of the largest section of the crowd... Sponsored by Arnotts and Ireland OnLine, this page provided minute-by-minute live commentary of this year's All-Ireland final at Croke Park.
http://ireland.iol.ie/all-ireland

Alliance Party of Northern Ireland

The first political party in Northern Ireland to have an official home page on the Web. A very comprehensive compilation of Alliance people and policy, the latest edition of Alliance News and links to other political and governmental pages, with particular reference to liberalism and Northern Ireland. In true liberal fashion, the Northern Ireland links include one to a Web site with information on Sinn Féin.
http://solution.unite.net/customers/alliance/
Email: nwhyte@unite.net (Nicholas Whyte)

A.M. Services Chauffeur Drive

Listing of the transport services provided by this Dun Laoghaire-based family-operated chauffeur drive company with 25 years experience, including 24 hour service countrywide, meeting passengers and conveying them to their destinations, in a Mercedes S class, stretched limousine, Daimler or Rolls Royce.
http://www.internet-eireann.ie/amservices/ams.html
E-mail: ams@internet-eireann.ie

AMEV Insurance

AMEV specialise in home, motor and travel insurance. Their page includes links to details on what they offer in each of these areas.
http://www.internet-eireann.ie/Adnet/clients/amev/html/amev.htm
Email: amev@iol.ie

An Taisce

Web page of The National Trust for Ireland — links include Treasure Ireland, living heritage, events, Ireland's blue flag beaches, young

---

Please email changes or new URLs to mnugent@internet-eireann.ie or mnugent@iol.ie
Please also email me if you have difficulty locating a page, and I will try to assist you.

Le Louvre — http://mistral.enst.fr/~pioch/louvre | The URL File

reporters for the environment, Tailor's Hall and useful environmental and other contacts.
http://www.commerce.ie/ca/antaisce
Email: antaisce@internet-eireann.ie

Ancestral Videos
This Cork based business will provide you with your own personal video of your Irish Roots. They will trace your family history which will show aspects of Irish life in the parish of your forefathers, locate the home or ruin of the house where they were born, the school where educated and the games they played.
http://www.cis.ie/marketplace/av/

Anna Livia FM
Broadcasting on 103.8 MHz from 5pm to midnight and all day long at weekends, Anna Livia FM is Dublin's Public Service Radio station. Includes programme schedule details, contact information, and a general introduction to the concept of community radio.
http://slarti.ucd.ie/annalivia/index.html
Email: rah10@ail.amdahl.com

Anuna
A group of singers and instrumentalists, formed by Michael McGlynn to promote and develop Irish music. Their Web page includes details of the group's repertoire and forthcoming concerts. If your computer can play sound (.wav files), you can download a clip from "Media Vita", the opening track of their first album.
http://www.dsg.cs.tcd.ie/dsg_people/skenny/anuna.html
Email: skenny@dsg.cs.tcd.ie

Archaeology Ireland
A full colour, quarterly magazine aimed at the wider public who are interested in archaeology. Its Web page includes links to an online database which contains 231 excavation reports from 1993 and to sample articles from the Summer 1995 edition. It also has subscription charges and details of back-issues of Archaeology Ireland.
http://slarti.ucd.ie/pilots/archaeology/

Ardagh Heritage Centre
Details of the Heritage Centre exhibition which outlines the history of Ardagh village in the Irish midlands, five miles from Longford, National Tidy Towns winner 1989 and winner of several European Awards.
http://www.internet-eireann.ie/Intermark/ardagh.htm
Email: carrick@internet-eireann.ie

Aritech Ireland Security Systems
Details of home and industry security panels, diallers and sensors provided by Aritech, including infra red detectors, movement sensors, sirens and bell boxes, fire panels and shock sensors. You can also sign the Aritech visitors book, email an R&D member, try some other interesting links or download a test file.
http://www.iol.ie/~aritech/
Email: aritech@iol.ie

Armagh Observatory
Links include planetarium information, pictures through the planetarium telescopes, a mail order catalogue, information on Armagh city, Armagh Observatory and other planetarium Web page addresses.
http://star.arm.ac.uk/planet/planet.html
Email: ipg@star.arm.ac.uk

Arnotts
Arnotts has been established in Dublin for 150 years, with its flagship store in Henry Street. As official sponsors of the Dublin Gaelic Football Team since 1991, their Web page allowed readers to send messages of support to the Dubs in the run-up to the 1995 All-Ireland football final against Tyrone, along with — on the day — live online commentary of the match minute by minute.
http://www.iol.ie/arnotts/dubs/arnotts.html

ArtServices
A Belfast based organisation which provides a range of services to the arts and cultural sector. Their pages will in time cover the whole range of arts and cultural activities in Ireland, with entries indexed and cross-linked.
http://slarti.ucd.ie/pilots/artservices/about.html

Artwork Unlimited
Services offered by this Dublin based company which provides a comprehensive range of services to the advertising and print industry in Ireland, including typesetting, design, on-

---

Note: As the Web is continually evolving, some of these pages may have moved or expired. Ask for details at the email address — if listed — which is less likely to have changed.

| The URL File | **Lego Home Page — http://legowww.homepages.com/** |

site desktop publishing, media advertising and print management.
http://www.iol.ie/~artwork/
Email: artwork@iol.ie

Athlone RTC
See RTCnet entry.

Atlantic Island
Published by Morigna MediaCo Teoranta, Killala, Co. Mayo, Atlantic Island is a subscription based online service providing information and news on property, people and work in Ireland.
http://www.internet-eireann.ie/atlanticisland/
Email: morrigan@virtualimpact.ie

Atlantis Internet Services
Based in University College Cork, Atlantis provides Telnet and Web consultancy, HTML authoring and design, graphic origination and manipulation, Web site design and technical troubleshooting.
http://atlantis.ucc.ie/services/flyer.html
Email: inquiries@atlantis.ucc.ie

Aubrey Fogarty Associates
An established Advertising Agency, Aubrey Fogarty's Web page includes planned links to a listing of their current clients, an executive profile of the agency, and advice with practical assistance for your business about how the Internet could be used by you.
http://www.virtualimpact.ie/AFA/
Email: info@virtualimpact.ie

Baileys Original Irish Cream
A marriage of fresh Irish cream, Irish spirits, Irish Whiskey and natural flavours. The Baileys page includes links to some interesting facts about Baileys, a cocktail list of interesting ways to try Baileys, a selection of dessert recipes, a selection of Baileys latest advertisements and a competition with some fun prizes.
http://ireland.iol.ie/resource/baileys/
Email: charris@baileys.iol.ie

Ballyfermot Senior College
A comprehensive Web page which includes guidelines for applicants for post-secondary PLC courses, and links to details on courses in all departments including Popular Performing Arts, Animation, Art and Design, Business and Computing, Media and Broadcasting, Electronics and Engineering, Social Care, Hotel, Catering and Tourism.
http://www.iol.ie/~scb/index.html
Email: scb@iol.ie(Jerome Morrisey)

Bank of Ireland Group Treasury
This Web page includes a Daily Market Commentary with spot and forward rates, spot rates vs the Irish pound, FRA rates and interest rates; a Weekly Update and a Monthly Market Bulletin with exchange rates, three month interest rates, and update on Ireland, forecasts and an economic diary, an Irish Chart Book with information by market sector, and a 30-strong country briefing covering Australia to Thailand.
http://www.treasury.boi.ie/
Email: info@treasury.boi.ie

Barnardo's
A voluntary child care organisation which works to advance the welfare of children and families in Ireland, in consultation with statutory and other agencies and in partnership with parents, focusing especially on those experiencing disadvantage or whose well-being is at risk. To this end Barnardo's provides a range of family support services in Dublin, Limerick and the Midlands, details of which are covered in their Web page.
http://www.iol.ie/~barnardo/
Email: Barnardo@iol.ie

Bates Ireland Survey Results
This Dublin advertising agency conducted a study of Irish attitudes to everyday living compared with those held by the British and the Americans. So where do we in Ireland stand today on a number of key questions? Are we materialistic — or do we seek the simple life? Is the concept of marriage alive and well, and who is boss in the home? The answers to these questions and others may well surprise you...
http://www.iol.ie/resource/bates/

Please email changes or new URLs to mnugent@internet-eireann.ie or mnugent@iol.ie
Please also email me if you have difficulty locating a page, and I will try to assist you.

Lesbian & Gay Pride — http://www.flavour.co.uk/flavour/pride | The URL File

BBC

Not technically an Irish page, but we do spend a lot of time watching it (the BBC on the telly, that is, not their home page). Everything you want to know about the BBC, including links to information on many popular programmes.
http://www.bbcnc.org.uk/

Beamish & Crawford

Step 1: Select a tulip-style glass. Use a clean glass every time. The correct serving temperature for Beamish is 8 degrees c... You'll have to check out this page for Steps 2–5 on pouring Beamish stout the Irish way. An Aardvark-created page, it also includes links to details on taking Care of your Beamish, a history of the brewery, and a special report on Beamish & Crawford.
http://www.aardvark.ie/beamish/

Beaumont Hospital

Includes facts about the Beaumont Hospital, general hospital information (including visiting hours and internal telephone listings for patients services, clinical support departments, laboratory and X-ray department), the hospital computer department Web page, and some useful pointers to other medical sites.
http://www.iol.ie/~beaumont/
Email: beaumont@iol.ie

Beech Lodge

Includes directions, facilities and rates for Beech Lodge guest house, Dunshaughlin, Co. Meath, a large modern dormer bungalow in rural setting beside Black Bush golf course and close to Fairyhouse Racecourse and Tattersalls Equine Sales Complex.
http://www.internet-eireann.ie/ipi/guest/beech/index.html

Benown House

Details and rates for staying at this Athlone based guesthouse, with details on local golf courses, fishing facilities, restaurants and other places of local interest such as Athlone Castle, Clonmacnoise and trips on the Shannon.
http://www.iol.ie/~patbyrne/welcome.html
Email: patbyrne@iol.ie

B.H. Associates Ltd

Services offered by this Dublin and Shannon based information technology management and software development company, including VOCAL, a complete hardware software package that provides a new way for remote users (customers, sales reps etc.) to access your computer system using nothing but their ordinary telephone.
http://www.iol.ie/~bhasocsn/welcome.html

Big Bear Sound Ltd

A Dublin based supplier of audio equipment for recording studios and artists. This page will include up-to-date information on the latest technologies available to people in the recording profession.
http://www.internet-eireann.ie/web1/bigbear/

Big Issues (Belfast)

The Big Issues is a magazine which campaigns on behalf of the homeless and unemployed. Its Web page includes details of the articles covered in the current edition, contact details for more information or if you're interested in selling The Big Issues, and a feedback form for providing information necessary for processing purchasing and information requests.
http://slarti.ucd.ie/pilots/bigissues/index.html
Email: macrob@inttelec.mcl.co.uk

Biotrin International

A biotechnology company founded by Dr Cormac G. Kilty in 1992 and based in Dublin, Biotrin company currently markets over 80 products throughout the world in two key markets; biomarkers to improve organ care, and tests in clinical virology. Distribution is through agencies and subsidiaries in Germany, France and a newly opened office in the USA and the UK.
http://www.internet-eireann.ie/Biotrin/index.htm
Email: bdalton@biotrin.ie (Barbara Dalton)

Blarney Woollen Mills

Includes links to pages on tourism, culture, history and an online catalogue of goods including crafts — handmade pottery and wrought iron — gift items such as a solid silver replica of the Cross of Durrow, traditional Claddagh ear-rings, a cloth-bound miniature version of the Book of Kells, plus mens and

---

Note: As the Web is continually evolving, some of these pages may have moved or expired. Ask for details at the email address — if listed — which is less likely to have changed.

| The URL File | **Liberal Democrats — http://www.compulink.co.uk/libdems/** |

ladies fashion and sweaters and more. There is also an online order form if you decide you want to purchase something.
http://www.ireland.net/marketplace/blarney/
Email: blarney@ieunet.ie

Bluffer's Guide to James Joyce
Bloomsday: if you can't beat 'em, bluff 'em — the lazy reader's guide to James Joyce. Includes extra-credit anecdotes on Ulysses, Finnegans Wake, Portrait of the Artist etc., which can also be used for face-saving emergencies or knock-'em dead exit lines...
http://www.paddynet.ie/create/writing/joyce.html

Bodhrán Page
Includes a calendar of bodhrán-related events, pictures of bodhráns and beaters, history of the bodhrán, buying or making a bodhrán, caring for a bodhrán, various styles and techniques of bodhrán playing, a bibliography of bodhrán books, instructional videos and tapes, competitions on the bodhrán, a complete index to all the documents in this site and, of course, a list of bodhrán jokes.
http://www.panix.com/~mittle/bodhran.html
Email: mittle@panix.com (Josh Mittleman)

Bohemians FC (unofficial page)
Maintained by Brian Crean, the Bohs homepage includes links to match fixtures, results and reports plus all sorts of information on the club and its players.
http://brianc.maths.may.ie:8001/bohs/bohs.htm
Email: bcrean@maths.may.ie

Boner, PJ & Co. Ltd
Details of services provided by this Dublin based company, including control systems (design, manufacture, installation and commissioning of electrical, electronic, pneumatic, P.L.C. and computerised systems), weighing, service and projects (pre-installation inspection and calibration, installation, loop checks and final commissioning).
http://www.internet-eireann.ie/bdi/home/pjboner/index.html

Breenson Limited
Details of quality souvenirs and giftware including ceramics, gift textiles, gift foods, leisure wear, knitwear, perfumes, toiletries and more offered by this Dublin based international wholesalers.
http://www.iol.ie/~breenson/
Email: Breenson@iol.ie

Broadcom Éireann Research
A telecommunications management company with a track record in large-scale international project management, the Broadcom Web pages include links to company details, partners & projects, the company's technical journal, employee profiles and internal information (accessible by staff only).
http://www.broadcom.ie/
Email: webmaster@broadcom.ie

Burren College of Art
Details of study programmes available in the Burren College of Art in painting, drawing, photography and sculpture, information on college amenities and housing, a faculty profile plus some information on the Burren itself.
http://www.iol.ie/~burren/
Email: burren@iol.ie

Burren Fish Products
Have Lisdoonvarna Smoked Salmon delivered right to your door world-wide, vacuum packed to seal in its freshness and encased in a stylish presentation box. Burren Fish Products will address it for you, enclose your personal message and deliver it by express courier to almost anywhere in the world!
http://www.iol.ie/resource/produce/burren/burrenfish.html
Email: burren.fish@iol.ie

Bruckless House
Accommodation details for staying in this comfortable 18th century Georgian house in Co. Donegal, with traditional farmyard, Connemara ponies and Irish draught horses. Local history a speciality.
http://iol.ie/~bruc/bruckless.html
Email: bruc@iol.ie (Clive Evans)

BTiS
The Business and Technical Information Serrvice, BTiS, is an extension of the University of Limerick Library & Information

---

Please email changes or new URLs to mnugent@internet-eireann.ie or mnugent@iol.ie
Please also email me if you have difficulty locating a page, and I will try to assist you.

Service and is specially tailored to the needs of business, industry and the professions. A wide range of information needs can be addressed using the resources of the University of Limerick Library or by accessing over 4,000 local and worldwide online databases. BTiS is a member of the European Information Researchers Network, EIRENE.
http://www.ireland.net/marketplace/eirene/BTIS.html

Byrne, Paul & Co. (Accountants)
Accountancy, audit and taxation services. Their Web page targets people thinking of setting up a business in Ireland, and offers to guide them through the maze of tax registrations, tax returns, banking facilities, company formation, grant applications, annual audit and filing requirements etc., leaving them to go on about their business.
http://www.internet-eireann.ie/byrne/
Email: pbfca@internet-eireann.ie

Cairbre House
Details and rates for holidays in Cairbre House in Dungarvan, County Waterford, built by the Duke of Devonshire in 1819 and located in its own grounds on the Colligan River estuary.
http://www.internet-eireann.ie/ipi/guest/cairbre/index.html

Canada Life
A password-protected Web page.
http://www.canadalife.ie/

Cantrell and Cochrane
At time of writing, this site comprises a test home page for Club Orange while the real one is under construction, with a competition where you can win a Club Orange t-shirt and a link to the Pepsi home page.
http://www.iol.ie/~mnolan/index.html
Email: mnolan@iol.ie

Carlow RTC
Information on the college, courses, staff and non-curriculum activities, plus a very interesting page on Carlow and surrounding

areas including famous Carlow people, the 1798 Rebellion, Kildare Failte, Carlow Eigse Festival and Kilkenny Arts Week. Also includes a picture of Carlow in the 1890s from the Lawrence collection (Carlow was the first town in the British Isles to be lit by electricity). See also RTCnet entry.
http://www.rtc-Carlow.ie/
Email: kinsella@akmac (Austin Kinsella)

Careers Register
An online jobs page from this specialist recruitment company with over twenty five years experience in the fields of database development, MIS management, networking, software programming, software engineering, systems programming, systems support, technical sales and operations.
http://www.internet-eireann.ie/Ireland/careersr.html
Email: careers@iol.ie

Carr Golf & Corporate Travel
A Dublin based destination management company marketing its services to international corporations, travel companies, or individuals to assist in determining what resorts, or combination of resorts in Ireland will suit a particular group. The Web page includes links to details of the Carr family, Irish resorts and Ireland's greatest golf courses.
http://www.internet-eireann.ie/web1/carrgolf/
Email: carrgolf@internet-eireann.ie

Catholic Information Centre
A central directory and repository of all data on Internet that reflect the Magisterium or authoritative teaching of the Catholic Church, using hyperlinks to Internet sites, home pages documents and discussion groups. Links include What's New, Papal visit, issues and facts, teachings of the Catholic Church, services, resources and periodicals.
http://www.catholic.net

Celtic Quest
Prices and details for seven-day Irish holidays, plus links to a page with information on accommodation, getting around, activities and comments from satisfied clients.
http://www.internet-eireann.ie/ltw/cquest/
Email: cquest@itw.ie

Note: As the Web is continually evolving, some of these pages may have moved or expired. Ask for details at the email address — if listed — which is less likely to have changed.

The URL File	**Macintosh Web Tools — http://www.arpp.sfu.ca/tools/**

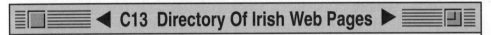
Chaloner, Hugh
Home page of Hugh Chaloner, who does non-linear editing for a company called diVa using Fractal Design's Painter, Adobe's Photoshop, Equilibrium's DeBabelizer and Avid's Media Composer.
http://www.iol.ie/~hugh00/
Email: hugh00@iol.ie

Chapman Flood Budget Analysis
An online analysis of the Budget, with information on personal allowances, tax bands, Residential Property Tax, deeds of covenant, relief on transfer of business assets, Capital Gains Tax, Vehicle Registration Tax and Mortgage interest and VHI reliefs.
http://www.ireland.net/marketplace/chapmanflood/
Email: info@ieunet.ie

CharterNET
The home page of the Institute of Chartered Accountants in Ireland, offering members a variety of Internet services. Links include ICAI contacts, President's Line, Annual Residential Conference for ICAI Members, Library Online, Accountancy Ireland, CPD Professional Development, Irish Taxation Developments, PracticeNET, Business Network, ICAI Publications & Sales, Careers Placement Service, District Societies, StudentNET and Accounting Information on the Internet.
http://www.icai.ie/
Email: charternet@icai.ie

Chemisolv
A leading provider of chemical technology to a wide range of industries, Chemisolve is part of the Serv-Tech group. Its Web page includes links to details on the Chemisolv concept, who is who in Chemisolv, a company profile, associated companies, and sectors in which Chemisolv operates including water and wastewater, hydrocarbon processing, paper and pulp, Nutrisolv, research and development and applications.
http://www.eirenet.net/marketplace/Chemisolv/

A Child's Guide to Good Food
M.B. Hill celebrated her 60th year in this incarnation by studying printing and sitting her professional examinations, and by writing, designing and illustrating her first book. "A Child's Guide to Good Food" is a collection of the rhymes she used to say to her own children — this page includes some samples and other details on the book.
http://www.internet-eireann.ie/Adnet/clients/mbhill/html/mbhill.htm

Chris De Burgh
A link from the Avalance Records home page, this includes details of the latest Chris de Burgh releases (at time of writing, "High On Emotion — Live From Dublin" including "The Lady In Red", "Missing You", "Don't Pay The Ferryman", and "Spanish Train").
http://www.bonaire.com/av18.html
Email: avalanche@bonaire.com

Christies Property Services
An Irish owned Estate Agency operating one of the largest letting services in the Dublin region, with close links to a number of accommodation agencies in France. Their Web page includes links to details of their services in Ireland including residential lettings, property available for rental, property management, property for sale, residential sales, business and commercial sales, relocation assistance and valuations.
http://www.internet-eireann.ie/ipi/christie/index.htm
Email: rosgraerin@internet-eireann.ie

Circa Art Magazine
A journal of contemporary visual culture, published quarterly in colour, Circa includes a range of articles on theory, criticism, history, new technologies and cultural practice, as well as news, reviews and work by contemporary Irish artists. Circa is funded by the Arts Council of Northern Ireland and An Comhairle Ealaíon. Includes links to recent features including the history of Irish participation at the Venice Biennale, and a review of the IMMA Glen Dimplex Awards exhibition at the Irish Museum of Modern Art.
http://slarti.ucd.ie/pilots/circa/

City.Net Guide to Ireland
City Net Express in Portland, USA, maintains a series of Web pages with information on

---

Please email changes or new URLs to mnugent@internet-eireann.ie or mnugent@iol.ie
Please also email me if you have difficulty locating a page, and I will try to assist you.

Map Browser — http://pubweb.parc.xerox.com:80/ | The URL File

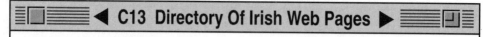

nearly 1,000 cities worldwide. Its Ireland page has links to pages on Cork, Dublin, Galway, Tralee and Waterford, along with links to various other pages with Irish-related material.
http://www.city.net/countries/ireland/
Email: info@city.net

City.Net Guide to Dublin
Includes links to Richard Bolger's page on famous Dublin people, Chris Zimmermann's Dublin Pub Guide, a guide to Dublin by four TCD students (Damien Byrne, Dominic Byrne, Mary Giblin and Louise Jevens), plus pages on the Bedrock Theatre Company and the Strawberry Beds.
http://www.city.net/countries/ireland/dublin/
Email: info@city.net

Claddagh Films
A small, independent film production company based in Galway. Their Web page gives details of their film and television projects which are in various states of production, plus interviews with Claddagh Films cast, crew and staff, clippings from newspaper and magazine articles, and links to information on film festivals around the world, indexed by country.
http://www.iol.ie/~claddagh/
Email: WebMaster@claddagh.ie

Clannad (unofficial page)
"With haunting songs, mesmerizing vocals, and a captivating sound that blends elements of traditional Irish and contemporary music, Clannad continues to occupy a unique place in the modern musical world..." Maintained by John Whatmough, links from the page include Who is Clannad?, Clannad discography, Clannad articles and interviews, Clannad graphics, Clannad fan clubs and information and other links related to Clannad.
http://www.empire.net/~whatmoug/clanhome.htm
Email: whatmough@mv.mv.com

Clár Cinn do Ráth Cairn
Homepage of the Meath Gaeltacht Community. Links include an Scéal 1935–1995, an Gaeltacht, an túdarás, chomharchumann Rath Cairn, saoire teanga agus chultúir samhradh 1995, gaeltacht Baile Ghibb agus mapaí, plus an English language version.

http://www.iol.ie/~obrienp/rathcarn/

Classic Hits 98FM
The largest independent radio station in the Irish market, Classic Hits broadcasts to the greater Dublin area. Their page includes links to details on the station, programme information, contests and promotions, Pat And Elaine's Morning Crew Page, sales and marketing and other Irish sites. You can email Pat and Elaine, Mark Cagney, Jim O'Neill or the 98FM Newsroom.
http://ireland.iol.ie/resource/98fm/
Email: hutton@iol.ie (Ken Hutton, Station Manager)

Cleary, James and Sons
Properties on offer from this Castlerea, County Roscommon based auctioneer and valuers, including bungalows, cottages, residential properties, licenced premises and farms in the Roscommon and Galway areas.
http://www.ireland.net/marketplace/homehunters/jc/
Email: cleary@property.ie

Cleo's Wearable Art
With shops in Dublin and Kerry, Cleo's specialises in clothes made from natural fibres — wool and linen — of Irish origin. Many of their designs are drawn from Ireland's past. This online brochure includes photographs, price lists and an online order form to obtain a printed brochure.
http://www.internet-eireann.ie/Adnet/clients/cleo/html/cleo.htm
Email: cleo@internet-eireann.ie

Client Solutions Ltd
This Cork based company aims to become the leading provider of tools, training, consultancy and development expertise in the client end of client–server technology, as this is the interface between the users and the implementation of their business requirements. Services include basic sale of development tools and associated training consultancy, project management of a client–server project and development of the application used in the project.
http://www.cis.ie/marketplace/client-sol/
Email: client@client-sol.ie

Note: As the Web is continually evolving, some of these pages may have moved or expired. Ask for details at the email address — if listed — which is less likely to have changed.

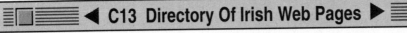
CMI Cable

Details of services offered by this cable television network operating company with cable and MMDS (Wireless Cable) franchises in urban and rural communities in Ireland, with in excess of 50,000 subscribers.
http://www.screen.ie/Business_connect/cmi/ index.html
Email: stevek@iol.ie

Columb Brazil Auctioneers

Properties on offer from this Kildare based auctioneering firm, include (at time of writing) two residential farms with many features including gate lodge, court yard and outoffices.
http://www.ireland.net/marketplace/ homehunters/cb/
Email: brazil@property.ie

CompuStore

Details of special offers, current finance deal on Packard Bell computers and technical support for repairs and upgrades.
http://www.iol.ie/compustore/
Email: compustr@iol.ie

Computer Access

A new facility in Dublin offering individuals and companies hourly access to PC's, software, printers, one-to-one tuition sessions, access to the Internet, and Internet training.
http://www.iol.ie/~caccess/
ciara@iol.ie

Computer Entertainment Ireland

C.ENT.I is the first Irish company to use multimedia to promote Irish-originated music and entertainment. Their online 'magazine is devoted to showcasing Irish talent — everything from music to fashion designers.
http://starbase.ingress.com/cent/
Email: webmaster@centi.ie

Computer Placement

Jobs on offer from this Dublin based supplier of specialist information technology personnel with vital computer skills. Page includes a company overview, company database and details of services to candidates.
http://www.internet-eireann.ie/Ireland/ cmplment.html
Email: cpl@iol.ie

Computer Products / Power Conversion Europe

Comprehensive details of products and services offered by this multinational manufacturer of standard and custom-designed electronic products and subsystems for power conversion, industrial automation and other real-time systems applications.
http://www.eirenet.net/marketplace/cpipce/ index.html

Concern

An international voluntary non-governmental organisation devoted to the relief, assistance and advancement of people in need in less developed areas of the world. Their home page includes links to information on current activities and how you can help.
http://ireland.iol.ie/biz/concern/
Email: concernd@iol.ie

Conflict Resolution in Ireland

This page, one of the United States Institute of Peace Web pages, contains Internet sources concerning conflict resolution in Northern Ireland, divided into categories including committees, organisations and programmes, documents, journals, news clippings, press releases, general reference, Usenet newsgroups and mailing lists.
http://witloof.sjsu.edu/peace/n-ire.html

Connemara Properties

Details of properties on offer from this Clifden, County Galway based auctioneers, including guest houses and private residences.
http://www.ireland.net/marketplace/ homehunters/conn/
Email: connemara@property.ie

Contech Medical International

US based multinational firm which has recently opened a manufacturing supply and medical contract packaging facility in Ireland.
http://www.iol.ie/~burke/contech.html
Email: burke@iol.ie

Cork Aviation Centre

Details of this new air taxi and charter company, based at Cork Airport, which can fly five passengers in comfort to any destination

---

Please email changes or new URLs to mnugent@internet-eireann.ie or mnugent@iol.ie
Please also email me if you have difficulty locating a page, and I will try to assist you.

Media Studies — http://www.aber.ac.uk/~dgc/media.html | The URL File

in Ireland, the United Kingdom or continental Europe and return the same day to Cork.
http://www.aardvark.ie/cac/
Email: bj@eirenet.net

Cork Business Innovation Centre
Services offered to convert an idea into a project, and the project into an industrial reality, based on promotion of entrepreneurship, evaluation and selection of entrepreneurs and projects, development of managerial skills, innovation and technology assistance, marketing aid and access to financing.
http://www.eirenet.net/marketplace/corkbic/
Postmaster@corkbic.com

Cork Campus Radio
Details about Cork Campus Radio, one of Ireland's first college radio stations, which began broadcasting in July 1995 to serve the students of both University College Cork and Cork Regional Technical College. Includes links to programming schedules and photographs of the CCR DJs.
http://atlantis.ucc.ie/ccr/campusradio.html
Email: radio@atlantis.ucc.ie

Cork Chamber of Commerce
A comprehensive and well-designed set of Web pages, this includes links to information about the Chamber and why to join it, the Chamber's 1994 Annual Report including the Council and Committees for 1994/95, the President's statement, visitors, functions, receptions and events. Also includes a link to the European Information Centre home page.
http://www.eirenet.net/cork/ccc/
Email: ccc@cork.com

Cork Heritage Park
An Atlantis Internet Services page, this includes details of exhibits and admission rates for the Cork Heritage Park, which was founded in 1993 to offer a varied and interesting introduction to aspects of Cork heritage that range from local ecology to the region's rich maritime heritage.
http://atlantis.ucc.ie/heritage/park.html

Cork Internet Services
Offers the full range of Internet connectivity services in the south of Ireland. It is a joint venture between Access Technology (Ireland) Ltd and IEunet Ltd — the page includes links to CIS marketplace, entertainment and leisure, Irish links, international links and usage figures.
http://www.cis.ie/
Email: webmaster@cis.ie

Cork RTC
See RTCnet entry.

Cornafest House Fishing
Run by Lottie and James McGerty, Coranfest Farmhouse in Carrigallen, Co. Leitrim, provides fishing holidays by some of the finest all-year round, coarse fishing waters in Europe, lying between the two major river systems of the Shannon and the Erne. You can visit at least 50 lakes, within a 30 minute drive.
http://www.iol.ie/~pwright/corn/
Email: ctcaeo@iol.ie

Cranberries (unofficial page)
Unofficial home page, with lyrics to Ode To My Family, I Can't Be With You, Twenty One, Zombie, Empty, Everything I Said, The Icicle Melt, Disappointment, Ridiculous Thoughts, Dreaming My Dreams, Yeats' Grave, Daffodill Lament and No Need to Argue.
http://www.ama.caltech.edu/~phil/cranberries.html

Crock of Gold
Maintained by Internet Presence Ireland, this site aims to reflect Ireland's place in both Europe and the world and to display all this small island nation has to offer the international community. The page has links to details on property, tourism, myths and legends, lifestyle, agriculture, bloodstock and computer services, plus Karl's Bazaar, a professional directory and an actors' register.
http://www.internet-eireann.ie/ipi/
Email: rosgraerin@internet-eireann.ie

Cylon Controls Ltd
Cylon Controls design and manufacture state of the art building energy management systems. Their Web page includes links to technical bulletins, product information, macro library and sample strategies.
http://www.internet-eireann.ie/Euromall/ireland/cylon/cylon.html

---

Note: As the Web is continually evolving, some of these pages may have moved or expired. Ask for details at the email address — if listed — which is less likely to have changed.

| The URL File | Mental Health — http://freenet.msp.mnus/ip/stockley/mental_health.html |

Dakota Packaging

Details on this Dakota Group company, which produces packaging for a wide range of market leaders and supplies worldwide markets in health-care, food, pharmaceuticals, cosmetics, confectionery, computers, tobacco and consumer durables.
http://www.internet-eireann.ie/ambar-www/dakota.html
Email: feargal@dakota.internet-eireann.ie

Daly, Dominic J.

Descriptions and photographs of properties on sale from this Cork based real estate agency.
http://www.aardvark.ie/dominic-j-daly/

Dara Records

From this site, you can order a range of cassettes or CDs from some or Ireland's most popular recording artists, including Mary Black and Frances Black.
http://www.iol.ie/irishmall/dara/
Email: irishmus@iol.ie

DECexecutive Recruitment

Provides recruitment services in the IT industry on a world-wide basis with a database of personnel and connections to many other recruitment agencies database. Their page includes an overview of DECexecutive, details of positions available and skills required, and you can submit CV information online.
http://www.internet-eireann.ie/Jobs/recruit/decexec.htm
Email: decexecutive@siog.enet.dec.com

Delaney Marketing Consultants

Details of services offered by this Dublin based destination management company which specialises in planning and organising special events, meetings, conferences and special interest programmes, including golf.
http://www.internet-eireann.ie/ltw/dmclli/dmc/
Email: dmc-lli@itw.ie

Deloitte & Touche Ireland

One of the largest accounting and management consulting firms in Ireland and world-wide, with 56,000 people in 122 countries. Their page has links to details on the company's background, clients and services plus other Deloitte & Touche international Web pages.
http://www.internet-eireann.ie/dttirl/
Email: paraic.hegarty@dtti.team400.ie

Delphi Software

Provides high quality software services and attained ISO 9002 certification in 1993. Employs over 90 IT professionals and has gained preferred supplier status to a number of blue-chip companies locally. Their Web page includes links to details on information technology services, technical authoring services and software test services. You can also send them your CV online.
http://ireland.iol.ie/resource/delphi/
Email: delphi@iol.ie

Democratic Left (unofficial page)

Aims to deal with issues of interest to the Left from an Irish and European perspective. Planned contents in late 1995 included pages on the divorce referendum, crisis pregnancies and women's right to choose, setting a new agenda for Northern Ireland, economic issues, Democratic Left in Government, and news of European, national, local and by-elections.
http://www.tiac.net/users/jimanne/index.html
Email: jimanne@tiac.net

Discover The Best Of Ireland

Very comprehensive listing of tourist attractions and facilities in Ireland. There are links to details on more than 150 towns or areas (Abbeyleix, Achill Island, Adare, Ahakista, Aldergrove, Aran Islands etc.) with information on national grid reference, county, nearest airport, distances, tourist sights and amenities, hotels, restaurants, pubs and more. Also includes a picture gallery of images of Ireland and travel information on getting to Ireland, and foreign language versions of the page in Français, Deutsch and Italiano.
http://www.iol.ie/~discover/welcome.htm
Email: discover@iol.ie

DIT Web Marketing Survey '95

An online questionnaire which forms part of Robert Abbey's undergraduate thesis at the Dublin Institute of Technology, aiming to

Please email changes or new URLs to mnugent@internet-eireann.ie or mnugent@iol.ie
Please also email me if you have difficulty locating a page, and I will try to assist you.

Movie Clichés — http://www.well.com/user/vertigo/cliches.html | The URL File

develop a demographic profile of those Web users who fill in the questionnaire, to document online purchasing behaviours of respondents and to determine the general attitude of Web users to e-commerce.
http://www.internet-eireann.ie/dit/survey.htm
Email: rabbey@internet-eireann.ie

Dublin City Libraries
Dublin Corporation Public Libraries have introduced Internet access facilities for members of the public. A volunteer public access group will assist the Library service in preliminary research aimed at increasing access to the service by a wider audience. ILAC Centre library staff will be pleased to assist you if you have specific research or business or recreational needs, which can be satisfied via the Internet.
http://ireland.iol.ie/resource/dubcitylib/
Email: Dublin.Central.Lib@iol.ie

Dublin City University
DCU offers 17 full-time primary degree programmes, a range of postgraduate taught programmes, postgraduate research degrees, part-time, evening programmes and distance education programmes. This page has links to the various Web sites maintained by the DCU School of Computer Applications, Centre for Software Engineering, School of Electronic Engineering and Centre for Teaching Computing. Other information will be added as other Schools and units contribute. Also includes a link to a DCU Star Trek home page.
http://www.compapp.dcu.ie/DCU_home.html
Email: webmaster@compapp.dcu.ie

Dublin Gliding Club
The Dublin Gliding Club operates from Gowran Grange, Naas, Co. Kildare. They usually fly on week-ends only but summer courses are also organised. The club has a reciprocal membership agreement with the Ulster Gliding Club where they traditionally spend their Easter holidays. Visiting pilots are welcome (special rates, bring your logbooks along) as well as non-pilot visitors (day or month membership available).
http://www.dsg.cs.tcd.ie/dsg_people/ sloubtin/DGC.html
Email: Sylvain.Louboutin@dsg.cs.tcd.ie.

Dublin Institute for Advanced Studies
A statutory corporation established in 1940 under the Institute for Advanced Studies Act of that year. The Institute pursues fundamental research in specialised branches of knowledge and trains advanced students in methods of original research. The page has links to information on the Institute's three schools — the Schools of Celtic Studies, Theoretical Physics and Cosmic Physics.
http://atlas.cp.dias.ie/Welcome.html
Email: web-master@cp.dias.ie

Dublin Institute of Technology
Includes links to details on the colleges, faculties and departments of the DIT including DIT Kevin Street (electronic and electrical engineering, maths, computer science, chemistry, biology, physics, photography, baking), DIT Bolton Street (mechanical & structural engineering, architechture, surveying & building, printing), College of Marketing and Design (marketing, design graphics, 3D design, retailing & distribution), College of Commerce (business studies, business information systems, law, communications & broadcasting, journalism), College of Catering (catering operations, hotel management and tourism, food sciences and environmental health, social sciences) and College of Music (music, drama).
http://147.252.133.152/
Email: bredmond@dit.ie (Barry Redmond)

Dun & Bradstreet
From this page you can request online a free Business Information Report, a once-off trial for debt collection and a breakdown of the Irish Marketing database. Also includes details of Dun & Bradstreet publications such as "The Marketing Guide to Ireland", the new "Business Ratings Guide", "Stubbs Gazette" and "Dun & Bradstreet's Business Education Service".
http://www.iol.ie/resource/dandb/
Email: dbradire@iol.ie

Dun Laoghaire Senior College
Links include information on courses in Accounting Technician IATI, Certified Public Accounting CPA, Financial Services Certificate

---

Note: As the Web is continually evolving, some of these pages may have moved or expired. Ask for details at the email address — if listed — which is less likely to have changed.

The URL File | **Millenium UK — http://www.milfac.co.uk/milfac/**

IOB/UCD, Hairdressing and Beauty Care and Computer Technology.
http://www.iol.ie/~scdl/

Dundalk RTC
See RTCnet entry.

Dunne, Matt, Auctioneers
Details of properties on offer from this Portarlington based auctioneer, including bungalows, farms and other residences.
http://www.ireland.net/marketplace/ homehunters/dunne/
Email: info@ieunet.ie

EFL International Distribution Ltd
Services provided by this international freight forwarding company, including company profile, new Switzerland service, air freight and imports and exports worldwide to and from Ireland.
http://www.iol.ie/resource/imi/efl/
Email: chris@efl.ccs400.ie

Eglington Manor, Dublin
Details and prices for staying at Eglington Manor, close to Donnybrook Village near Dublin city centre and within walking distance of the RDS showgrounds and conference centre.
http://www.eire.com/turas/EglingtonManor/ index.html
Email: web@eire.com

EI5DI
PC contest logging programmes for you to download. Includes links to what's new, what users say and reference manual.
http://www.iol.ie/~okanep/index.html
Email: okanep@iol.ie

Eirenet
Cork based Internet Service Provider. This page has links to Eirenet pages including Chemisolv, Cork Aviation Centre, Cork Business Innovation Centre, Cork Chamber Of Commerce, Cork International Film Festival, Ossian Publications, Synergy

Workshop and Aardvark Internet Publishing.
http://www.eirenet.net/
Email: webmaster@eirenet.net

Eleanor McEvoy
Includes a biography and discography plus information on forthcoming gigs, contact information, image and sound archives, and a songbook including lyrics of her hits from "Only a Woman's Heart" onwards.
http://www.internet-eireann.ie/Dojo/eleanor/
Email: bobby@dojo.internet-eireann.ie (Bobby Gibbson, Web page maintainer)

Electronic Frontier Ireland
Formed in 1994 to promote digital communications and protect the rights of those using them, EFI aims to promote the use of the Internet and bulletin board systems, to help improve Irish communication structures, to clarify the laws surrounding computer usage, and to safeguard electronic privacy. The EFI Web pages include activity, membership and contact information plus a good online summary guide to using the Internet in Ireland.
http://www.maths.tcd.ie/~efi/
Email: efi@efi.ie
(Secretary: Antóin O Lachtnáin)

Ellis, Tommy, Studios
A recording studio that does everything from radio commercials to television and video soundtracks, Tommy Ellis Studios has a large client base from both within the country and from abroad. They have worked on a number of major projects including U2 " Zoo TV " Video wall inserts, documentaries and commercials, the Perry Como TV Christmas Special and the videomixes for the Garth Brooks' singles "Ain't Goin' Down Till The Sun Comes Up" and "The River". Their home page includes details on the studios, ISDN world-wide connections, their equipment list and their sound FX library.
http://ireland.iol.ie/resource/tellis/
Email: locky@iol.ie (Locky Butler)

ELTA
Details of services offered by this English Language Tuition and Accommodation service based in County Galway.
http://www.interact.ie/marketplace/interact/ elta.html

Please email changes or new URLs to mnugent@internet-eireann.ie or mnugent@iol.ie Please also email me if you have difficulty locating a page, and I will try to assist you.

Mirsky's Worst — http://turnpike.net/mirsky/Worst.html | The URL File

Emerald Star
Details of cruising holidays on the Erne and Shannon with the Emerald Star hire fleet of over 200 cruisers strategically based at three cruiser stations along these waterways.
http://www.misty.com/ulysses/vip/tourism/ emerald/emerald1.htm

Envirotone
Envirotone provides re-manufactured laser toner cartridges — savings of up to 40% can be achieved — details on this Web page.
http://www.iol.ie/~enviro/index.html
Email: enviro@iol.ie

Equinox
Provides computer graphics services for businesses. Details on their Web page about computer presentations and multimedia, internet Web page design and administration and, for the small office/home PC user, image scanning, text scanning, and PC to Mac to PC disk and file conversion.
http://www.internet-eireann.ie/equinoxweb/ index.html
Email: equinox@internet-eireann.ie

ERA-Maptec
Provides consultancy services to the minerals and petroleum exploration community, specialising in preparation and interpretation of remote sensing imagery. Their Web page includes links to details on their departments and the services they provide.
http://www.internet-eireann.ie/Adnet/ERA-Maptec/
Email: webmaster@mekquake.era.ie

Eurokom
An Internet Service Provider whose system can be accessed from Local Access Nodes in most major cities around the world. Customised services include high speed file transfer and database facilities.
http://www.eurokom.ie/www/service.html
Email: help.desk@eurokom.ie

European Freight Information Services
This Dublin based service is currently under development — at time of writing, the Web page includes details in French of European services.
http://www.iol.ie/~efis/
Email: efis@iol.ie

European Information Centre
The Euro Info Centre, in association with Cork Chamber of Commerce, is now using the Internet as a way of disseminating EU information. Includes links to the newsletter of the Euro Info Centre, a two page summary of EU happenings updated weekly and an alphabetical index to European Union funding opportunities.
http://www.eirenet.net/ccc/eichome/ internet1.html
Email: ccc@eirenet.net (Tara Dennehy)

Euromall
A directory of business, shopping, software, leisure, computers, sports, and other interests. Currently has listings on Ireland, the UK, Germany, Italy and France. Irish pages in the directory include Cylon Controls energy management systems, Roslyn jewellery and crafted leather, Tipperary Crystal, The Store (Royal Tara China, ceramics, Irish ties, scarves, sounds of Ireland), Comcom Systems computer software, plus links to sites of Irish interest.
http://www.internet-eireann.ie/Euromall/ index.html
Email: Euromall@internet-eireann.ie

Europa Groupware
Company profile includes details of services such as development of custom written software, development of macros to allow the automation of repetitive tasks, integration, presentations and multimedia, template design, consultancy and product support. The home page also has links to recent case studies of EGL projects.
http://www.iol.ie/~europa/egl.htm
Email: europa@iol.ie (Alex Porter)

EIRENE
The European Information Researchers Network, EIRENE, is a professional organisation representing 56 Information Brokers from the EC, EFTA and Eastern European countries. It aims to promote

---

Note: As the Web is continually evolving, some of these pages may have moved or expired. Ask for details at the email address — if listed — which is less likely to have changed.

| The URL File | Multimedia — http://www.acm.uiuc.edu/rml/ |

contacts between European information brokers, increase access to information and develop information brokerage as a commercial activity, whilst working towards raising the quality of service to clients. EIRENE members in Ireland include Aisling Information Systems Ltd and the University of Limerick Business & Technical Information Service.
http://www.ireland.net/marketplace/ eirene/Foreword.html

Everyman Computers
As well as selling computers, Everyman are specialists in upgrades, repairs, manufacture of custom systems and network solutions. Their page includes company and price details plus links to other places of interest on the Web. There is also a link to a special offer form which you can print out and use to get a 10% discount on selected items.
http://ireland.iol.ie/resource/everyman/
Email: Everyman@iol.ie

Everson Gunn Teoranta
A software and publishing company supporting minority-language (including Irish, Welsh) communities since 1990, founded by Michael Everson and Marion Gunn. Links to details of Apple and other software, fonts, publications and work in International Standards.
http://www.ucd.ie/~mgunn/egt-homepage-en.html
Email: everson@internet-eireann.ie or mgunn@irlearn.ucd.ie

Executive Recruitment Consultants
Details of this Dublin based recruitment consultancy specialising in management and professional recruitment, covering a wide range of manufacturing, sales and marketing, and service industries.
http://www.internet-eireann.ie/Ireland/erc.html

Eyecon Eyewear
Summary of services available from this Dublin based dispensing optician and sunglasses specialists, which include 500 different styles of sunglasses and designer frames.
http://www.adnet.ie/Adnet/clients/eyecon/ html/eyecon.htm

FAS Loughlinstown
Details of training courses, multimedia courses and evening courses run at the FAS Training Centre in Loughlinstown.
http://www.iol.ie/fas/
Email: fasltcde@iol.ie

Fastfreight
This Bray based company offers a shipping service, including a daily groupage service to and from the UK and Europe, a nationwide distribution and warehousing service. They are sole Irish agents for Boston Logistics USA.
http://www.internet-eireann.ie/freight/rooney/
Email: fastfgt@internet-eireann.ie

Fingers Unlimited
Details of typesetting service run by Anne O'Neill of Glasnevin, Dublin.
http://www.iol.ie/~fingers/
Email: fingers@iol.ie

First National Building Society
An informative and well-designed page. Includes links to information on services offered (savings, home loans, personal loans, commercial mortgages etc.), plus the Beehive Club for Net Kids with interactive stories for your children and a link to a page with items of environmental interest.
http://ireland.iol.ie/resource/imi/first/
Email: fnbs@iol.ie

Firstaff Recruitment
Details of jobs on offer from this Dublin based personnel consultants firm specialising in the areas of technical and computers, financial services, marketing and sales, administration and warehousing.
http://www.internet-eireann.ie/Ireland/ fstaff.html
Email: firstaff@iol.ie

Fitzpatricks' Castle Hotel
Details, facilities and rates for staying at this four star castle hotel, originally built in 1741 as a family mansion, on Killiney hillside overlooking Dublin Bay.
http://www.misty.com/ulysses/hotels/fitzptrk/ fitzptrk.htm

Please email changes or new URLs to mnugent@internet-eireann.ie *or* mnugent@iol.ie
Please also email me if you have difficulty locating a page, and I will try to assist you.

Myers-Briggs Personality Test — http://sunsite.unc.edu/jembin/mb.pl | The URL File

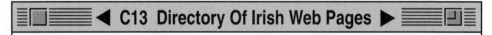

FM104

Broadcasts to Dublin City and County under the regulations of the Independant Radio & Television Commission. Their home page has programme schedule details and links to pages with information on station promotion details, Planet X Show, 9 to 5 Club, Strawberry Alarm Clock, 9 Most Wanted, Bee-Bop Sunday and Network Radio News. Plus you can leave a message online for the very popular late-night Chris Barry Show.
http://www.dublin.iol.ie/fm104/
Email: fm104@iol.ie

Focal Point

These pages combine up-to-date information and marketing activity on computer related hardware companies, software companies, news, conferences, FTP support sites, publications and jobs.
http://www.iol.ie/~indigo/
Email: indigo@iol.ie

Forbairt

Established by the Irish Government to facilitate the development of Irish industry, to encourage technology and innovation and to provide technology services to all firms. Their Web page includes an organisation chart and an information request form, plus details on Forbairt regional offices and Forbairt technology services now on the Web.
http://www.netc.ie/forbairt.html
Email: fitzgeraldj@netc.ie (Jackie Fitzgerald)

Forfás Network

The role of Forfás is to advise on and co-ordinate policy for the development and promotion of industry, science and technology in Ireland. Their Web page is an online version of Forfás Network, a quarterly newsletter published by Forfás. The first edition has a special focus on science and technology. Future issues will report on a wide range of policy matters, nationally and internationally, of relevance to industry in Ireland.
http://slarti.ucd.ie/pilots/forfas/

Fortnight Magazine

An Independent Review of Politics and the Arts published in Belfast, its Web page includes contact information, a sample leader article,

and an analysis of the peace process.
http://slarti.ucd.ie/pilots/fortnight/
Email: macrob@inttelec.mcl.co.uk

Forum for Peace and Reconciliation

Includes links to pages with background information on the Forum, its terms of reference, members and proceedings so far, plus press releases, key Forum documents and publications.
http://www.internet-eireann.ie/web1/forum/
Email: forum@internet-eireann.ie

Fusio

A Dublin based multimedia development company whose Web pages, marketed under the name WEB1, include The Forum for Peace & Reconciliation, Carr Golf & Corporate Travel, Big Bear Sound and Larry Hogan.
http://www.internet-eireann.ie/web1/welcome
Email: mmug@internet-eireann.ie

Futura Marketing

Bray based company with a Web authoring partnership with ITCo (see separate entry on ITCo).
http://www.internet-eireann.ie/futura/
Email: futura@villapacis.internet- eireann.ie

 ## GAA (unofficial page)

Headlines, results and fixtures, plus a brief history of the GAA and links to GAA home pages in the following counties so far: Antrim, Armagh, Cavan, Donegal, Dublin, Kildare, Killkenny, Louth, Longford, Wexford, Wicklow, Kerry, Galway, Leitrim and Roscommon.
http://www.compapp.dcu.ie/GAA/
gaa_home.html
Email: c2mking@compapp.dcu.ie

Gaelic Homepage

A Web site devoted to the language and culture of the Gaels. Includes a comprehensive series of links to pages on Gaelic languages, the Celts and the six Celtic languages, the Gaelic language mailing list and electronic

---

Note: As the Web is continually evolving, some of these pages may have moved or expired. Ask for details at the email address — if listed — which is less likely to have changed.

| The URL File | **Natural Law Party — http://www.fairfield.com/nlpusa/NLP_HOME.html** |

library, Sabhal Mór Ostaig, the Soc. Culture.Celtic newsgroup FAQ (Frequently Asked Questions), Gaelic language books and tapes, RTÉ radio (Internet) news, the Irish Times, Gaelic music and general information.
http://sunsite.unc.edu/gaelic/
Email: elessar@physics.unc.edu
(Seán O Mìadhacháin)
or godfrey@itc.icl.ie (Godfrey Nolan)
or jw@conan.rti.org (John Walsh)

Gaelic Lessons Online

Sabhal Mór Ostaig, a Gaelic speaking college on the Isle of Skye, has been given a grant of £5000 by the University of the Highlands and Islands Project to put Gaelic lessons on the Internet. When completed, the lessons will be at the "Blasad Ghàidhlig" (a taste of Gàidhlig) level, and will have sound samples.
http://www.smo.uhi.ac.uk/beurla/
Gaelic_lessons.html
Email: caoimhin@smo.uhi.ac.uk
(Caoimhín P. O Donnaíle)

Galway Aquaconsulting

Details of the services provided by this company in fish related activities comprising fish farming, processing and marketing, working with associated companies in the west on aquatic environmental projects.
http://www.iol.ie/~gac/

Galway RTC

Information on the RTC's management, schools (including Business & Humanities, Engineering, Hotel & Catering, and Science), courses and other services such as library facilities and adult and continuing education. Also includes links to Peadar O'Dowd's informative page on "Galway, City Of The Tribes" and Pat Folan's Connemara Home Page. See also RTCnet entry.
http://ns.rtc-Galway.ie/
Email: pscannel@aran.rtc-galway.ie
(Paul Scannell)

Genealogy Resources on the Web

Maintained by Paddy Waldron at TCD, this page contains links to the FAQ (Frequently Asked Questions) on genealogy and the Web, a guide to genealogical research in Ireland, the Irish-Canadian List, Web pages set up by the North of Ireland Family History Society, details of documents in the UK Public Record Office dealing with emigrants, and some links to information on his own family.
http://www.bess.tcd.ie/genealog.htm
Email: pwaldron@tcd.ie (Paddy Waldron)

Genesis Project

Belfast based Internet Service Provider whose Web page includes links to contents, the company, Northern Ireland information, trade centre, community, users and customers.
http://www.gpl.net/
Email: webmaster@www.gpl.net

Gerry Ryan Tonight

The Tonight Show on the Internet — the programme which, aided by Gateway 2000 computers, has for the most part eliminated paper from its set. The Web page includes links to audio greetings from, and pictures of, Gerry Ryan and the programme's production team, plus schedule details for coming shows and a chance for you to contribute your opinions.
http://ireland.iol.ie/grt/
Email: grt@rte.ie

Gilroy Automation

Contact details for this company based in Dublin, Cork and Belfast which provides a wide range of instrumentation for the measurement, recording, monitoring and control of any industrial or monitoring process.
http://www.internet-eireann.ie/bdi/home/
gilroy/index.html

Glounthaune Newsletter

Only two editions online (April and May 1995) but an excellent example of how a local community (in this case Glounthaune, County Cork) can let the world know what they are doing. Sample links include Golf Classic, Confirmation, Cork–Cobh Rail Line, Draft Development Plan, Tidy Towns 1995, Village Fair, First Communion, Classified Section, Social and Personal and Review of Events.
http://www.cis.ie/leisure/glounthaune/

Go Ireland

Ireland for the great outdoors — order the Go Ireland full colour brochure, which includes links to pages on hidden Kerry, independent

---

Please email changes or new URLs to mnugent@internet-eireann.ie or mnugent@iol.ie
Please also email me if you have difficulty locating a page, and I will try to assist you.

walking, cycling safari, Go As You Please activities for softies and short breaks
http://www.ireland.net/marketplace/go-ireland/
Email: goireland@fexco.ie (Anne Coffey)

Goodbody Stockbrokers
Includes information on Goodbody's services and an Irish Bond Market Review, with planned links to a commentary on the Irish stockmarket and individual stock data.
http://www.internet-eireann.ie/Goodbody/
Email: goodbody@virtualimpact.ie

Grange Community College
Comprehensive details of this Donaghmede based community college, including links to details on school management, educational courses, school uniform, remedial and special education, college chaplain and guidance counsellor and extra curricular activities.
http://www.iol.ie/~frcost/
Email: frcost@iol.ie

Green Party
The first Republic of Ireland political party on the Web. Its page has contact information for the Green Party's elected representatives, Patricia McKenna MEP, Trevor Sargent TD and former Dublin Lord Mayor John Gormley plus links to pages on the Green Party's policies on transport, agriculture and food, neutrality and international affairs, local government reform and decentralisation, Green economics and women.
http://ireland.iol.ie/resource/green/
Email: greenparty@iol.ie

Greenane Riding Centre
Offers the horse-riding enthusiast nice hacks in County Kerry woods, strands or mountains, and also riding or jumping lessons in an outdoor arena supervised by a BHS qualified instructor. Complete one week travel arrangement including accomodation in nearby B&B or hotel is available.
http://www.iol.ie/~joepl/
Email: greenane@iol.ie (Joep Laumans)

Guinness — The Local
A set of animated Web pages, which begin with the contents of a pint vanishing before your eyes. There are also links to free competitions, and to other places of interest on the Web, a chance to send online feedback about what you would like to see at "The Local", plus you can download a free Guinness screensaver if your computer is a PC.
http://www.itl.net/guinness/

Harris, Tony, Services
Offers multiple services to clients including software support for Thesaurus Software, installation and training, Internet training, first aid for hardware, customised payroll utilities and a wide range of services to importers and exporters alike in areas of customs clearance for third country traffic and Intrastate returns for EC trade.
http://www.internet-eireann.ie/harris/
Email: tom@tonyharris.internet-eireann.ie
(Tom Horan)

Hartmanns Jewellers
Products and prices from Hartmanns of Galway, one of the few stockists in Ireland for Rolex watches, now also offering exclusive Claddagh rings handcrafted in Galway.
http://www.interact.ie/marketplace/interact/
hartmann/index.html
Email: hartmann@iol.ie

HEA Archives Server
This server is operated by the HEAnet Network Operations Centre and is managed by BTiS at the University of Limerick. It is used to host a wide range of archived material (software and information) that can be downloaded via the Internet, mostly mirrored from primary sites throughout the world.
http://www.hea.ie/
Email: nis@ul.ie or
archive-admin@www.hea.ie

Henry Street — A Trip To Ireland
Starting with "Go n-éirí an information highway libh!", Caroline Von B. has compiled an excellent page of Irish interest from the perspective of a Dutch visitor to the country. Includes her own visitor's guide to Ireland — "A Trip Through your Eire" — along with some of her writings and poems about Ireland, and

---

Note: As the Web is continually evolving, some of these pages may have moved or expired. Ask for details at the email address — if listed — which is less likely to have changed.

a very comprehensive set of links to almost a hundred pages of Irish interest at home and abroad, agus as gaeilge.
http://huizen.dds.nl/~vonb/hs-index.html

Heraldic Gifts
Details of services provided by a Dublin based heraldry company whose directors include former Dublin Lord Mayor John Gormley.
http://www.misty.com/ulysses/vip/shop/ herald/herald.htm
Email: jgormley@iol.ie

Hillebrand, J.F.
Major multinational shipper of wines and spirits, page includes links to details on service, Irish growth, how the company can help you and history of J.F. Hillebrand.
http://www.iol.ie/~karlmo/welcome.html
Email: karlmo@iol.ie

HMV
Includes details on coming gigs and shows for which HMV are ticket agents, new album and single releases, new videos available at HMV, games, charts, t-shirts, soundtracks and more plus an online form for you to give feedback. Also links to Top Ten lists for albums, classical albums, Irish albums, jazz albums, games, videos, Irish videos, soundtracks and t-shirts plus Top Twenty lists for Irish singles and UK singles.
http://www.iol.ie/resource/hmv/

HomeNet
New Internet Service Provider a subsidiary of Horizon Computing (see separate entry on Horizon).
http://www.homenet.ie/

Hot Press On The Net
An online version of the long-running music and current affairs magazine edited by Niall Stokes with contributions from Liam Mackey, Declan Lynch, Bill Graham, Eamon McCann, Nell McCafferty, Gerry McGovern, George Byrne and many others. Current and recent editions are available to subscribers only at an annual subscription of £25. Older back issues (6 months) are publicly available free.
http://www.iol.ie/hotpress/
Email: hotpress@iol.ie

Horizon Computing
Horizon is a European distribution, training and consultancy organisation specialising in the area of Open Systems and Internetworking technologies. Their Web page includes links to details on SunOS and Solaris training, Cisco training courses, consultancy services, call centre services, product distribution and employment opportunities within Horizon.
http://www.horizon.ie/
Email: webmaster@horizon.ie

House Of Dojo
Includes links to the Web pages of Dublin radio stations Radioactive 95.5 FM and Radio Caroline, the radio show Radio Net Ireland, the Eleanor McEvoy Home Page and the Militant Labour Home Page.
http://www.internet-eireann.ie/Dojo/
Email: joel@dojo.internet-eireann.ie

IBEC
Web page of the Irish Business and Employers Confederation. Includes links to comment and analysis on the major issues affecting business, employers, employee and industrial relations, economic affairs, research and information, trade and industry affairs, European and international affairs, sectors and associations, social affairs and specialist services, further information and feedback.
http://www.iol.ie/ibec
Email: tdonohoe@iol.ie

ICL
The ICL Information Technology Centre page includes links to details of current ITCentre projects, how to become an ITCentre customer and job opportunities at the ITCentre.
http://www.itc.icl.ie/
Email: webmaster@itc.icl.ie

ICS Building Society
This wholly owned subsidiary of the Bank of Ireland Group provides residential mortgage finance and savings and investment services. Their web page includes a brief history of the

---

Please email changes or new URLs to mnugent@internet-eireann.ie or mnugent@iol.ie
Please also email me if you have difficulty locating a page, and I will try to assist you.

Newbie's Net Guide — http://www.hip.com/franklin/franklin.html   The URL File

ICS, plus links to information on mortgage products and rates, a step-by-step guide to getting your own home, information on savings and investments and a mortgage health check. Their Web services will be available to residents of the Republic of Ireland, and when finalised will also detail a wide range of mortgage and investment options.
http://www.iol.ie/ics/
Email: icsbuild@iol.ie

IDA

"Ireland, which is a full member of the 340 million population European Union, is a politically stable, modern, low-inflation economy..." Information on what Ireland has to offer for companies considering an expansion in the European Union. Includes sections on financial returns, incentives, infrastructure, sub-supply base, human resources and investors in Ireland, with particular reference to healthcare, international services and financial services.
http://www.ireland.net/marketplace/ida/
Email: idaireland@ida.ie

IEunet

Ireland's first direct Internet Service Provider. Includes links to the Eunet home page (IEunet's European partner), the Irish Market for products and tourist information, IEunet's information launch pad for interesting sites on the Net.
http://www.ieunet.ie/
Email: webmaster@eunet.ie

Imagis Data Imaging

Details of services offered by this Cork based private consultancy firm specialising in structural geology, remote sensing, and GIS applied to mineral and oil exploration. These services are fully supported by the latest technologies in image, map, and report generation.
http://www.eirenet.net/marketplace/imagis/imagis.html
Email: markf@eirenet.net

Infograf

Working exclusively with Ireland On-Line, InfoGraf Web development offers a complete design, implementation and maintenance service to companies and organisations. Their Web page includes a FAQ (Frequently Asked Questions) file and a feedback form for further information.
http://www.iol.ie/infograf
Email: infograf@iol.ie

Infopoint Systems

A software development company based in Galway specialising in interactive multimedia touch screen information systems. Their Web site includes an overview of the company's history, people, products and services plus links to the pages of their commercial partners such as Microtouch, AT&T and Siemens Nixdorf.
http://www.infopoint.ie/
Email: WebMaster@infopoint.ie

Institute of Chartered Accounts of Ireland

See CharterNet entry.

Institute of Irish Studies

Runs residential courses at Trinity College Dublin. The Institute was designed to meet the growing demand from around the world for a whole range of third level and adult courses dealing with aspects of Irish life and culture. Links to details on courses including Monastic Odyssey, Ireland in Film and Drama, To Hell or Connaught, The Wonders of Myth & Legend From Ireland's Rich Celtic Heritage and Funny Peculiar or Funny Ha Ha: The Comic Tradition in Irish Literature.
http://www.internet-eireann.ie/iis/
Email: iis@iol.ie

Interact Internet Services

Details on how this Galway based company can help get you up and running on the Internet, design, locate and market your Web presence and provide training in Internet usage.
http://www.interact.ie/marketplace/interact/
info@interact.ie

Interlinked

A small Dublin based firm which gives simple advice to people who want to take advantage of the Internet. All aspects of using the Internet for communications are covered — technical,

---

Note: As the Web is continually evolving, some of these pages may have moved or expired. Ask for details at the email address — if listed — which is less likely to have changed.

The URL File | Newtwatch — http://www.cais.com/newtwatch

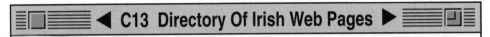
organisational and communications issues. The first needs assessment meeting is free.
http://www.eire.com/interlinked/index.html
Email: interlinked@eire.com (Antóin O Lachtnáin)

Internet Business Ireland
Develops Web sites in conjunction with Ireland On Line for companies who want to have an Internet presence, runs individual or group training courses and provides executive briefing sessions. Includes link to an online Irish Mall which markets and displays Irish goods and services.
http://www.iol.ie/resource/imi/travel/ibi.htm
Email: crowef@iol.ie (Fred Crowe)

Internet Eireann
Home page of one of Ireland's main Internet Service Providers. Includes links to pages on Internet-related issues, business and entertainment plus details on Internet Eireann usage statistics, activities and services.
http://www.internet-eireann.ie/
Email: admin@internet-eireann.ie

Internet Events Ltd
A company that provides Internet presence services plus a Web page with links to News Headlines On The Hour, a Chat Server, Sports Results, Previews and Reviews, English Premier League, Kids Corner, Terry Rogers Bookmakers, Fantasy Island Pictures and Charity Pages. And, if you don't think that's enough, they offer (promise?) to come round to your office, break all the handles off your cups, and nail your jackets to the wall.
http://www.internet-eireann.ie/i-events/
Email: internet-events@internet-eireann.ie

Internet Exchange
At time of writing opening soon in Dublin, the Internet Exchange will be a walk-in centre and café with access to the internet via approximately 25 PCs. The Exchange will offer training to individuals and groups on using the internet and other computer products.
http://www.iol.ie/~james/intex.html
intex@iol.ie

Internet HQ
See Underground Club entry.

Internet Presence Ireland
See Crock of Gold entry.

InterShamrock
Made real live shamrock available all over the world to Irish or would be Irish for St Patrick's day 1995. Look out for it again in 1996.
http://www.iol.ie/resource/imi/shamrock/
Email: info.shamrock@iol.ie (Ciara Crowe)

Iona Technologies
Home page of IONA Technologies, who released their core Orbix product in June 1993, which now ships worldwide and whose client base cover the telecommunications, manufacturing, finance, defense, medical, computing and research sectors.
http://www.iona.ie/
Email: info@iona.ie

Ireland America Web
Screengate's Ireland America Web aims to provide quick and easy access to all that Ireland and Irish America has to offer. Their Web page includes links to details on coming events, Ireland overview, Ireland America business, heritage and arts, sports and leisure, places to stay, travel connections and the Irish pub universe. The business section includes links to details on government facilities for business and Ireland's top 100 companies.
http://www.internet-eireann.ie/screengate/
Email: simon@screengate.ie

Ireland: The Internet Collection
This page contains links to various sources which contain information on Ireland. Includes a map of Ireland from the Xerox PARC map viewer, Tralee RTC's pages on the West Kerry Gaeltacht, the Virtual Tourist Guide to Ireland, Michael McGrath's Gaelic Football home page at Queens University Belfast, Tallaght RTC's Irish Law Page, latest photos of Ireland and Europe from the weather satellites and more.
http://itdsrv1.ul.ie/Information/Ireland.html
Email: webeditor@ul.ie

Ireland's Property Market
Links to pages with details of residential properties for sale from a selection of agents, including Columb Brazil Auctioneers of Newbridge Co. Kildare, Connemara Properties

---

Please email changes or new URLs to mnugent@internet-eireann.ie *or* mnugent@iol.ie
Please also email me if you have difficulty locating a page, and I will try to assist you.

The URL File

of Clifden Co. Galway, James Cleary & Sons of Castlerea Co. Roscommon, Matt Dunne Auctioneers of Portarlington Co. Laois, Hynes & Son MIAVI of Athlone Co. Westmeath, Ferris O'Reilly MIAVI of Naas, Co. Kildare, McCreery Auctioneers & Valuers of Kilkenny, Pat Mulcahy of Clare, Royal Auctioneers of Trim Co. Meath and Sothern Auctioneers of Carlow.
http://www.ireland.net/marketplace/ homehunters/
Email: rslevin@property.ie

Ireland's Weather Page
The meteorological situation over Ireland, some background information and pictures, plus short range weather forecasts (7 days) daily from yesterday to five days from today.
http://eisbahn.ucg.ie/msd_rpas.html

Irish American Partnership
A registered charitable organisation with established offices in Dublin and Boston. The Partnership's mission is the economic development of Ireland through investment in job creation and education. Their Web site includes links to some of their current literature.
http://www.internet-eireann.ie/Adnet/clients/ iap/html/iap.htm
Email: partners@internet-eireann.ie

Irish Breakfast
For only $35, you can order an Irish breakfast online (rashers, sausages, black and white pudding) and have it delivered to anywhere in the USA in less than 72 hours.
http://ireland.iol.ie/resource/imi/breakfast/

Irish Businesses
A very comprehensive online listing of Irish businesses on the Web, which you can search alphabetically or by category.
http://www.iol.ie/~aidanh/business/index.html

Irish Cycling
News and results of Irish cycling activities, plus information on Stage Race classification and rules plus contact information for the Federation of Irish Cyclists.
http://www.iol.ie/~sshortal/
Email: sshortal@iol.ie (Seamus Shortall)

The Irish Emigrant Archive

As the name suggests, a gopher menu of archive material from the Irish Emigrant, Ireland's first electronic mail newspaper. The archives run from 1987 to the present year. A sample edition (March 25 1995) includes comprehensive articles on St Patrick's Day in Washington and in Ireland, that week's developments in the Northern Ireland peace process, the reduction in the X case sentence, progress on the abortion information bill, bits and pieces, Northern Ireland news, the courts, industrial relations, politics and politicians, EU news, the Irish abroad, travel and tourism, conservation and the environment, education, music (including charts), books, deaths, business news, weather and sport. There is also an online order form.
gopher://gopher.iol.ie/11s/emigrant
Email: ferrie@iol.ie

Irish Incorporations
Includes links to information on Irish non-resident companies, incorporation costs and a sample Incorporation Application Form, and you are invited to contact them for a current list of shelf companies.
http://www.internet-eireann.ie/Irishcorp/ index.htm
Email: irishcorp@internet-eireann.ie

Irish Law Page
Maintained by Darius Whelan, who also runs a worldwide Irish Law mailing list. The Law Page includes the the Irish Law mailing list Frequently Asked Questions file, a search index for the Irish Law mailing list archives, Irish Law Messages at UCD Gopher, and links to other law-related materials including the Irish Constitution, the Framework Document, the Annual Report of the Ombudsman, a bibliography of British and Irish legal history from Aberystwyth, the Downing Street Declaration, Electronic Frontier Ireland, University College Dublin Law Faculty, Queen's University Belfast Law Faculty, Warwick Law Technology Centre and an alphabetical listing of law schools and law firms.
http://web.rtc-tallaght.ie/staff/academic/law/ irlaw.html
Email: dwh@staffmail.rtc-tallaght.ie or dwhelan@tcd.ie

Note: As the Web is continually evolving, some of these pages may have moved or expired. Ask for details at the email address — if listed — which is less likely to have changed.

The URL File	**Origami — http://www.cs.ubc/ca/spider/jwu/origami/html**

Irish Life International

Irish Life offers international investors security, confidentiality, tax efficiency and a selection of the world's best fund managers. This page invites you to contact them for further information.
http://www.ireland.net/marketplace/irish-life/
Email: irish-life@ieunet.ie

Irish Lottery Syndicates

Home page of a Galway based company which offers people abroad the opportunity to participate confidentially in the Irish National Lottery. If you win, you will be immediately notified by personal letter.
http://www.iol.ie/resource/lottery/
Email: ils@iol.ie

Irish Mall

An online shopping mall of Irish businesses — at time of writing included SpeechWriters, The Irish Breakfast, Dara Records, Poolbeg Group Services Ltd. and Ronnie Moore Paintings, with Gerrard Tailors, The Goldsmiths of Mira and Pub Paraphernalia Ireland soon to be online.
http://www.iol.ie/irishmall/
Email: crowef@iol.ie

Irish Music Page

Comprehensive set of links to information on dozens of Irish musicians ranging from Eleanor McEvoy and Sinead O'Connor to The Chieftains, Thin Lizzy and Rory Gallagher. Also includes an online Irish music quiz and links to pages about news, gig, reviews and clubs.
http://www.internet-eireann.ie/Dojo/musicbox/
Email: services@dojo.internet-eireann.ie

Irish Nanny Services

An established Dublin based company specializing in the placement of Irish nannies with families abroad. Their page includes details of services and costs and an online application form.
http://www.iol.ie/~aird/
Email: Aird@iol.ie

Irish Net Nippon

Web pages for and by the Irish community in Japan. The Irish Net Nippon was set up to use the information highway as a bridge between these two small island nations. Links include a mailing list, upcoming events, new resources, general news, working In Japan/Ireland and information on the various exchange programs available, Maureen and Brendan's Irish Traditional Music Pages and a sampling of Irish Web resources.
http://www.st.rim.or.jp/~jogama/inn/inn.html
Email: jogama@st.rim.or.jp (Jun Ogama)

Irish Newspapers on Microfilm

National Micropublishing's collection of Irish newspapers on microfilm is the largest available in the country and covers a wide spectrum of Irish Social History over a period of three centuries. Their page has links to available papers in three categories: National Daily Newspapers, Provincial Weekly Newspapers and Out of Print or Historical Papers. They also offer a printing and framing service for any page (16"x20" black and white) from any of the newspapers listed.
http://www.ireland.net/marketplace/natmicro/

Irish Orienteering

In orienteering you use a map and compass to find your way across unfamiliar terrain. A measure of success is commonly given by time taken to complete a given course or by the number of control flags found during a specific time allotment. This page includes Irish fixture and event lists plus links to other pages of orienteering interest including 10 Minute O-Tour of Ireland.
http://www.cis.ie/leisure/orienteering/
Email: Martin.Flynn@easylink.cis.ie

Irish Property Network

Details on buying properties in Ireland plus contact information for Irish Property Network members in Carlow, Clare, Cork, Donegal, Dublin, Galway, Kerry, Kildare, Kilkenny, Laois, Longford, Louth, Leitrim, Limerick, Mayo, Meath, Offaly, Roscommon, Sligo, Tipperary, Waterford, Westmeath, Wexford and Wicklow.
http://www.iol.ie/~property/
Email: property.iol.ie

Irish Punt Exchange Rate

Updated weekly. Next time we have an exchange rate crisis, you can check out what the punt in your pocket is worth in foreign

---

Please email changes or new URLs to mnugent@internet-eireann.ie *or* mnugent@iol.ie
Please also email me if you have difficulty locating a page, and I will try to assist you.

Palestine Information — http://www.alquds.org/ | The URL File

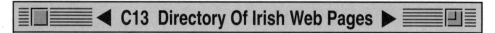
currencies from Argentina to Venezuela.
http://bin.gnn.com/cgi-bin/gnn/
currency?Ireland
Email: koblas@netcom.com (David Koblas)

Irish Recruitment Consultants
Details on this Dublin based recruitment
consultancy which supplies staff in the areas
of accountancy, technical and engineering,
computer and electronics, executives, sales
and marketing and secretarial staff.
http://www.internet-eireann.ie/Ireland/irc.html

Irish Rowing
Information on rowing in Ireland and regatta
dates and results. There is an index, listed by
province, with contact information for over sixty
clubs affiliated to the IARU. There are also links
to other rowing related Web pages including
one with e-mail addresses for rowing clubs
around the world.
http://www.ul.ie/Leisure/IrishRowing/
welcome.html
Email: gribbonj@ul.ie (Jane Gribbon)

Irish Science Fiction Association
The ISFA holds monthly meetings in Dublin
on the 1st Tuesday of every month. Their Web
page includes links to information on their
quarterly magazine "Phase", their artist's and
writer's workshop that meets monthly and their
monthly newsletter "First Contact".
http://arrogant.itc.icl.ie/ISFA.html
Email: VCanning@dit.ie
(Vincent Canning — Secretary)

Irish Smoked Salmon
This Ballina based business provides Irish
Atlantic Salmon from off the West Coast of
Ireland, delivered via DHL to anywhere in the
USA or Canada.
http://www.iol.ie/~fpirl/index.html

Irish Soccer Home Page
Includes links to this season's fixtures for the
Bord Gais National League Premier Division,
the results and fixtures for Ireland and Northern
Ireland's qualifying group for Euro 96,
information on the UEFA Cup and European
Cup Winners rounds which the Irish clubs took
part in and on the Ladies Soccer Colleges
Association of Ireland. There is also a link to a
page dedicated to the Northern Ireland
international side, and links to the Bohemians
and Shamrock Rovers home pages.
http://www.maths.tcd.ie/~thomas/soccer/
soccer.html
Email: thomas@maths.tcd.ie
(Thomas Bridge)

Irish Times On The Web
Between thirty and forty of the major articles
from The Irish Times from Monday to Friday
each week. Sections include front page stories
(including the "Inside The Irish Times"
summary), home news, sport, opinion,
editorials and letters, foreign news and finance.
There is also a comprehensive archive
database. The Irish Times and IEunet have
come together to provide this news service for
which there is no cost at present.
http://www.irish-times.ie/
Email: itwired@irish-times.ie
(for queries re electronic publishing)
or lettersed@irish-times.ie
(for letters to the Editor)

Irish Trade Board
The Government Agency responsible for
export promotion. Their range of services to
overseas buyers includes the provision of
information on sources of supply in Ireland.
They also plan itineraries and arrange
introductions to Irish manufacturers. Their
page includes links to details on Irish Trade
Board Offices and an offer to overseas
companies to let the Irish Trade Board
organise their trip to Ireland.
http://www.ireland.net/marketplace/irish-trade/

Irish Trade Web
Founded in 1995 by Micromedia to help
develop Internet based marketing, sales and
customer support solutions customised for
Irish businesses. Home page includes links to
client surveys and information, new and future
developments, doing business in Ireland and
some of ITW's client sites.
http://www.internet-eireann.ie/Itw/
Email: itw@itw.ie

Irish Xpress
Online archives of the daily paper produced
by the former Irish Press journalists, plus

---

*Note: As the Web is continually evolving, some of these pages may have moved or expired.
Ask for details at the email address — if listed — which is less likely to have changed.*

---

details of fundraising events which were organised during the dispute.
http://www.internet-eireann.ie/Adnet/xpress.htm

IRTC
The first Irish Government agency on the Web, the Independent Radio and Television Commission home page includes links to details on the IRTC itself, stations licenced by the IRTC, guidelines for the submission of applications for temporary broadcasting services, links to other sites, JNLR information, most recent IRTC news, codes of standards, practice and prohibitions in advertising, sponsorship, and other forms of commercial promotion broadcasting services, complaints procedure and advertising appendices.
http://www.iol.ie/irtc/
Email: irtc@iol.ie

IT Solutions
Details of this Dublin based company whose particular speciality is the grafting of modern customer service interfaces onto existing legacy systems, whatever the hardware or software platform — thus protecting often large investments in existing systems.
http://www.iol.ie/~itsols/
Email: itsols@iol.ie

IT's Monday
A weekly Irish publication, distributed by email, which specialises in computing, software and telecommunications news. The service is produced by Newsmail, a Dublin based company which promotes special interest journalism via new media. It is sold by subscription only and two types of licence are available. A personal licence, which is equivalent to a single-user software licence, is strictly limited to a single reader. A group subscription, equivalent to a multi-user software licence, authorises organisations to set up internal distribution lists.
http://www.ireland.net/marketplace/newsmail/
Email: deirdre@licensing.newsmail.ie
(Deirdre McGovern)

ITCo
This Dublin-based company is centred on designing and coding Web pages. They also specialise in training for the Internet. The company started in early 1995 and their clients include Thesaurus Software, Tony Harris Services, Paul Byrne and Co. (accountants), Futura Marketing, The Ultimate Freight List, Pat Nolan Freight Services and Fastfreight Limited.
http://www.itco.ie/itco
Email: it@itco.ie

Keane Mahony Smith
Links to details of properties on sale from Keane Mahony Smith auctioneers. The properties are situated mainly in the Cork, Roscommon, Tipperary and Kerry areas.
http://www.iol.ie/~kms/welcome.html
Email: kms@iol.ie

Kehoe and Associates
Links to details of properties on sale from Kehoe and Associates, mainly in the Wexford area.
http://www.ireland.net/marketplace/homehunters/ka/

Kenny's Bookshop of Galway
Specialising in new and antiquarian books of Irish interest, Kenny's is known throughout the world. Now, via the Web, you can browse and purchase from their on-line catalogue of over 25,000 titles. Other services available include an out of print search service, antiquarian maps and prints, Irish music and song on cassette, book binding, fine art and sculpture.
http://www.iol.ie/resource/kennys/
Email: kennys@iol.ie

Kenyon Antiques
Information on this traditional firm of family antique dealers, who have been in the business of supplying fine antiques for over two hundred years. Page includes a link to an online guide to the the Irish furniture at Malahide Castle.
http://www.koala.ie/KenyonAntiques/index.html
Email: markk@kenyon.iol.ie

Please email changes or new URLs to mnugent@internet-eireann.ie or mnugent@iol.ie
Please also email me if you have difficulty locating a page, and I will try to assist you.

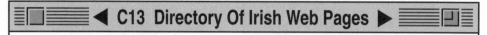

Kerna Communications

An Irish company which has been formed to market the leading edge skills developed over the past three years within the UCD projects group both nationally and world wide. Their page includes links to pages with information on Artservices, Circa arts magazine, Fortnight magazine, Big Issues magazine, Lakelands Country Breaks in Fermanagh and the Irish Arts and Cultural Information Service.
http://slarti.ucd.ie/pilots/kerna/
Email: alan@kerna.ie (Alan Byrne)

Kerry Home Page

How to get to County Kerry by air, ferry, rail or bus plus general tourist information on Kerry including places worth a visit, area and population, geography, economy, money, public transport, shopping, pubs, media, medical treatment, postal charges, telephone information. Also includes links to separate pages on Tralee, Tarbert, Killarney, Dingle, Castlegregory and the Maharees. The Tralee page includes a map and a short history of Tralee, plus information on Kerry County Museum, Tralee–Blennerville Steam Railway, Blennerville Windmill, Siamsa Tire, Fenit Seaworld Aquarium, The Aquadome, Festivals of Kerry including the International Rose of Tralee Festival, The Kerry International Summer School and Kerry Choral Union.
http://ns.rtc-tralee.ie/kerry.html
Email: lillis@bosheasrv0.rtc-tralee.ie (Deirdre Lillis) or paulc@staffmail.rtc-tralee.ie (Paul Collins)

King Fine Art

Sample images of reproduction prints of original paintings by leading Irish landscape artist Brendan Hayes, who is a member of the Association of Artists in Ireland. Prints on offer include The Ha'penny Bridge Dublin, Coliemore Harbour Dalkey, The Baily Lighthouse Howth, St Finbarr's Cathedral Cork, Kinsale, Gougane Barra, Ballydonegan Bay, Allihies, Dunguaire Castle Kinvara, Galway Cathedral, Doolin Co. Clare, Bunratty Castle, John's Castle Limerick, The Franciscan Abbey at Adare, Glendalough, The Sugarloaf from Roundwood and Greystones Harbour.
http://www.ireland.net/marketplace/fine-art/
Email: king-fine-art@ieunet.ie

Kinsale Home Page

Includes links to pages with information on Historic Kinsale (meander from a twelfth century church to a sixteenth century star-fort, taking in Ireland's first wine museum en route), Gourmet's Delight (restaurants, delicatessens and seafood shops plus the annual October Gourmet Festival), accommodation details and Kinsale Chamber of Tourism.
http://www.cis.ie/kinsale/
Email: brian.graham@easylink.cis.ie or 100275.3270@compuserve.com

Kinvara Smoked Salmon

How's about this for a sales pitch: Use your Internet connection to order by email some Irish Atlantic salmon, fished from the clean waters of Ireland's west coast, oak smoked in the traditional way at The Burren Smokehouse, and it will be delivered almost anywhere in the world within 48 hours by express couriers. Or try Irish whiskey flavour smoked salmon. Or honey and herb flavour smoked salmon. I ask you, is this the future or what?
http://www.iol.ie/resource/produce/kinvara/welcome.html
Email: by form on the Web page

Knickerbox Swimwear

Whether you are a serious swimmer or a sun worshipper awaiting those lazy Caribbean days (or possibly Dollymount strand, given the Summers we've come to expect now in Ireland), the Knickerbox page will let you choose the swimwear that suits your lifestyle.
http://www.internet-eireann.ie/Adnet/clients/knicker/html/knicker.htm

Koala Systems

A new Dublin based company providing a range of Internet based services, including Internet presence provision and consultancy. Their home page includes links to information on the services they provide.
http://www.koala.ie/
Email: emer@koala.ie

KT Cullen Environmental Noticeboard

Includes a company profile of KT Cullen, who provide independent consulting services to both private and public organisations covering

---

Note: As the Web is continually evolving, some of these pages may have moved or expired. Ask for details at the email address — if listed — which is less likely to have changed.

| The URL File | **Personalised Insults — http://www.preferred.com/~joey/insult.html** |

a wide range of environmental projects. Their Noticeboard page includes links to information on water quality standards and waste, water and environmental legislation. .
http://www.iol.ie/~ktcullen/
Email: (ktcullen@iol.ie)

Ladies Soccer Colleges Association of Ireland

Includes information on the combined colleges squads, the history of the association, the current situation and the future, and details of intervarsity, interprovincial, freshers and indoor tournaments.
http://www.rtc-carlow.ie/lsoccer/lsoccer.html
Email: kellym@rtc-carlow.ie (Myles Kelly)

Lakeview House
A Web brochure detailing the facilities available and the attractions located near these Bord Failte approved self-catering apartments in County Tipperary. Includes links to information on local amenities, tourist attractions and terms and conditions of rental.
http://www.iol.ie/~nbs/lakeview.htm

Laser Recycle Ireland
Using the slogan "Toner Cartridges that don't cost the earth", Laser Recycle Ireland is a Cork based electronic cottage business which recycles toner cartridges for laser printers using state-of-the-art computer systems. It has a client list that includes UCC, Cork RTC, Summit Technology and Cara Partners.
http://www.cis.ie/marketplace/recycle/
Email: laser@recycle.ie

Latchfords, Dublin
Details of services available and prices for staying at Latchfords serviced guest accommodation with self catering facilities in Baggot Street, Dublin.
http://www.misty.com/ulysses/bandb/dublin/latchfrd/latchfrd.htm

LearnNet
Web page for Network 2's new live interactive education series, presented by Cynthia Ní Murchú and produced by the Audio Visual Centre at UCD. Includes links to programme timetable and course material.
http://wwwavc.ucd.ie/LearnNet

Letterkenny RTC
See RTCnet entry.

Liffey Arts Research Centre
Situated in an 18th century mill on the banks of the River Liffey outside Naas in Co. Kildare, LARC's brief is to actively research the arts and sciences with a view to influencing the functional application of creativity in conceptual, economic and social processes.
http://www.internet-eireann.ie/larcweb/
Email: research@larc.internet-eireann.ie

Limerick RTC
See RTCnet entry.

Lurgan Holiday Apartments
Lurgan Holiday Apartments are situated 12 miles west of Galway City and 2.5 miles west of Spiddal village. Their home page includes links to information, prices, terms of hire and particulars plus an online order form.
http://www.interact.ie/marketplace/interact/lurgan.html

McCreery Auctioneers
Details of properties on sale, mainly in the Kilkenny area, from this Kilkenny based firm.
http://www.ireland.net/marketplace/homehunters/mccreery/
Email: info@ieunet.ie

McCullough, Lee & Partners
Details of this civil engineering practice who have worked on projects including the ILAC Shopping Centre, the AIB Bank Centre, Dublin Airport Control Tower, the Harcourt Centre and the IDA / Craig Gardner Headquarters, all in Dublin.
http://www.iol.ie/~lmp/index.html
Email: lmp@iol.ie

Please email changes or new URLs to mnugent@internet-eireann.ie or mnugent@iol.ie
Please also email me if you have difficulty locating a page, and I will try to assist you.

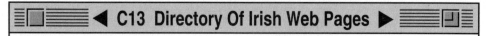

Mayo Editorial Services

Provide a unique combination of scientific background and long experience in publishing. Their technical editorial services include converting existing documents to Internet formats, editorial services for medical and scientific conferences, a full range of editorial services for scientific and technical publishers and camera-ready-copy preparation.
http://joyce.iol.ie/~mayoedit/mayohome.html
Email: mayoedit@iol.ie

Medical Resources

A list of links to medical resources online, maintained by Dr Joe Clarke of Summerhill, County Meath. Links include Global Health Center, Doctalk, Irish Medical Home Page from UCC, the Interactive Medical Student Lounge, the Virtual Hospital, Cyberspace TeleMedical Office, Muscular Dystrophy Ireland, Poisons Information Database and What's New.
http://www.iol.ie/~joec/med
Email: joec@iol.ie

Meehan, Sean and Co.

Details of properties on sale, mainly in the Donegal, Sligo and Leitrim areas, from this Bundoran based auctioneering firm.
http://www.ireland.net/marketplace/homehunters/sm/

Micromail Online Catalogue

Micromail, which is located in Cork, have put their entire computer book and software catalogues online for browsing. Their page includes links to the book catalogue, the software catalogue, ordering policy, contact details and a map of their shop location in Cork.
http://www.cis.ie/marketplace/micromail/
Email: 100066.752@compuserve.com

Micromedia

See Irish Trade Web entry.

Microprint

Information on Microprint, the Dublin based specialist printer of product and software manuals for international software publishers including Claris, Symantec, Logitech and Creative Laboratories.
http://ireland.iol.ie/~microprt/
Email: microprt@iol.ie

Militant Labour

A revolutionary socialist organisation. Their page includes online exerpts from their newspaper Militant Socialist, plus links to the works of Marx and Engels and to the illegal Dublin radio station Radioactive FM.
http://www.internet-eireann.ie/Dojo/rni.htm
Email: militant@dojo.internet-eireann.ie

Mitsubishi Computers Ireland

Mitsubishi Electric Corporation is part of one of the world's largest group of companies. All Mitsubishi Open Systems products are branded with the Apricot name. From links on their home page you can request information about any Apricot product in Ireland and participate in the Apricot User Survey.
http://www.iol.ie/mitsubishi/

Monaghan Mouldings

A company which specialises in decorative plasterwork, combining age-old traditional skills with new innovative procedures, their online catalogue includes pictures and details on cornices and ceiling roses.
http://www.internet-eireann.ie/mouldings/
Email: info@virtualimpact.ie

Montpelier Financial

Details of PC Market Eye, a service to give you live professional financial information direct to your PC at a low fixed cost. Includes an online form to order, to get further information or brochures, or to make an appointment to see a live demonstration of PC Market Eye in Dublin.
http://www.internet-eireann.ie/finance/
Email: netbiz@internet-eireann.ie

Moore, Ronnie, Paintings

Samples and an online order form for original watercolors from one of Ireland's well known watercolorist's, painted on handmade paper. You can also email your request for special commissions of your own choice.
http://www.iol.ie/irishmall/ronnie/
Email: crowef@iol.ie

Moresoft

This Dublin based company has over 10 years experience in computer applications, trading and consultancy. Their home page includes

---

Note: As the Web is continually evolving, some of these pages may have moved or expired. Ask for details at the email address — if listed — which is less likely to have changed.

The URL File	Playboy — http://www.playboy.com/

links to information on their consultancy, networking and training services, hardware and software products and employees.
http://www.internet-eireann.ie/ Moresoft_Home/
Email: moresoft@internet-eireann.ie

Morigna Mediaco

Details of Morigna Mediaco, a development of Morrigan Publishing, involved in the publication and distribution of specialist information books, local maps and guides and books on ancient Ireland including Irish folklore and mythology.
http://www.internet-eireann.ie/atlanticisland/ morrigan.html
Email: morrigan@virtualimpact.ie

Mulcahy, Pat, Auctioneers

Details of properties on sale, mainly in the Clare and Tipperary areas, from this Ballina based auctioneering firm.
http://www.ireland.net/marketplace/ homehunters/mulcahy/
eMail: mulcahy@property.ie

Murroe Holiday Cottages

Details of services and costs of staying in these self-catering cottages located in Murroe, Co. Limerick, a small village nine miles from Limerick city and forty minutes drive from Shannon Airport.
http://www.commerce.ie/cm/murroe/

Mountaineering Council of Ireland

These pages keep MCI members (over 3,000 people in almost 60 member clubs spread throughout Ireland) up to date with forthcoming happenings in the Irish mountaineering, rambling, hillwalking and rock climbing fields. Includes an online version of the MCI's quarterly magazine "Irish Mountain Log", a catalogue of MCI literature available at the University of Limerick Library which may be borrowed by MCI Members, a list of guides published by the MCI and links to other mountaineering resources.
http://www.ul.ie/~mci/
Email: murphyp@ul.ie (Paul Murphy)

MusicBase

MusicBase Provides information, advice and advocacy in matters affecting the Irish music industry. It also does consultancy work. Their page includes links to details on a sample promoter/venue artist agreement, music publishing, copyright, setting up an independent record label, running a charity concert, how to apply for entertainment visas for the USA, marketing a band or artist, soundproofing and presenting a demo.
http://www.internet-eireann.ie/wwwmb/
Email: musicbase@internet-eireann.ie

National Electronics Test Centre

NETC, a division of Forbairt, was established to provide electrical, electronic and communications testing and consultancy. Page includes links to details of NETC's test and consultancy services such as ISDN conformance testing, PSTN Telecoms testing, electrical safety testing and environmental testing.
http://www.netc.ie/
Email: webmaster@netc.ie

National Institute for Management Technology

The NIMT was set up under the Irish Software Programme for Advanced Technology, and is committed to ensuring that companies stay abreast of IT developments. Its Web pages give details on the objectives and portfolio of the Institute, plus a quarterly report and contact details.
http://www.nimt.rtc-cork.ie/nimt.htm
Email: romahony@nimt.rtc-cork.ie
(Ronan O'Mahony)

National Microelectronics Research Centre

Based in Cork, the NMRC was founded in 1981 and offers a full range of services to industry and is involved in leading edge electronics research with several major multinational electronics companies in the areas of IC process, packaging, devices and basic materials research. Several programmes are also funded under European research

---

Please email changes or new URLs to mnugent@internet-eireann.ie or mnugent@iol.ie
Please also email me if you have difficulty locating a page, and I will try to assist you.

| Poisons Information Database — http://biomed.nus.sg:80/PID/PID.html | The URL File |

programmes. Their home page includes links to details on Services to Industry, Organisational Contacts, Crossword Cheater, Smart Group — Ireland, Annual Report 1994, Latest News, Job Opportunities at NMRC and Scientific Report 1994.
http://nmrc.ucc.ie/
Email: admin@nmrc.ucc.ie

National Micropublishing Ltd
See Irish Newspapers on Microfilm entry

National Technology Park
Details on the National Technological Park in Limerick, Ireland, with links to a company directory, an About the Park section, a park bulletin and a park map.
http://www.commerce.ie/ntp/
Email: kellyo@shannon-dev.ie

National Telecommunications
Information on this Dublin based supplier of telephone and computer equipment. Also includes a link to the home page of Internet Services, an affiliate of the company, through which they design and provide Web pages.
http://www.internet-eireann.ie/telecom/
Email: mpark@iol.ie

NCB Stockbrokers
One of Ireland's leading stockbroking firms with an extensive range of domestic and international clients, NCB was acquired in 1994 by Ulster Bank Limited, a member of the NatWest Group. Linked pages from their home page include Bond Desk, Equity Desk, NCB Moneybrokers, Corporate Finance Private Clients and Research. There are also links to a Company Research Profile, Weekly Economic Research and Investment Focus.
http://www.iol.ie/resource/ncb/
Email: ncb@iol.ie

Newsmail
Newsmail delivers special interest news directly from their journalists to your computer through two email newsletters, IT's Monday and It's Europe. Both services sold by subscription only. Personal and multi-user licences are available.
http://www.ireland.net/marketplace/newsmail/
Email: deirdre@licensing.newsmail.ie

Niblicks Restaurant
Service and booking details for Niblicks, the restaurant at Fota Island Golf Club, situated a few minutes drive from Cork City.
http://www.aardvark.ie/niblicks/
Email: niblicks@eirenet.net

Norcontel
Information on this telecommunications consultancy based in Dublin with operations throughout Ireland, the UK, Europe, the Middle East and Asia. Norcontel provides consultancy in the converging fields of telecommunications and networking for both private system users and public telecommunications service providers.
http://www.iol.ie/~norcon/
Email: postmaster@norcontel.ie

North Dublin National School Project
The first Irish National School on the Web is a member of Educate Together. The NDNSP is a child-centred, co-educational, multi-denominational, democratically run school, located on the northside of Dublin. Its Web page includes links to pages created by 5th class students arising from their 1995 Science and Technology Week, covering topics such as local history, saving the broadleaf, flags along the Liffey, our garden in the NDNSP, history of the school and publications.
http://www.iol.ie/~ndnsp/
Email: ndnsp@iol.ie

Northern Ireland Civil Service
Information on central government and other public sector services in Northern Ireland, including bus and railway service details, the IDB publication "Best of Northern Ireland", details of the Community Information Network of Northern Ireland (CINNI),
http://www.nics.gov.uk/
Email: Webmaster@gnet.gov.uk

Northern Ireland Information Centre
Created and maintained by the Genesis Project, the NIIC Web page aims to provide an Internet window on Northern Ireland business, culture and tourism. Links include

---

Note: As the Web is continually evolving, some of these pages may have moved or expired. Ask for details at the email address — if listed — which is less likely to have changed.

The URL File	**Political Science — http://www.keele.ac.uk/depts/po/psr.htm**

recent and forthcoming events in Northern Ireland, the 12th of July parades, five day weather forecasts for Belfast and Derry, tourism information, cultural, social and sporting life, community groups, government in Northern Ireland, politics, business, education, religion and legal information.
http://www.gpl.net/niic/
Email: webmaster@www.gpl.net

Northern Ireland Visitors

Activity and travel tips for visitors to Northern Ireland, including information on the Giants Causeway, the Castles of Dunluce & Carickfergus, the Glens of Antrim, City of Armagh, Belfast, Ards Peninsula, Mourne Mountains, St Patrick's Country, Lough Erne, the Shannon–Erne Waterway, History of Derry, the Sperrin Mountains and more.
http://www.interknowledge.com/northern-ireland/index.html
Email: info@interknowledge.com

Norsk Data Systems

A high technology repair organisation located in Dublin, NDS provides repair and upgrade facilities for electronics systems companies. Their page includes a link to the company's online newsletter.
http://www.iol.ie/~ndsys/ndsys.htm
Email: ndsys@iol.ie

Northwest Connect

This regional Web server for the northwest of Ireland is brought to you by Screenphones of Sligo and Ireland On-Line. Links include business, White House Conference, region link and Social & Personal.
http://www.screen.ie/
Email: infosp@sligo.screen.ie

Northwest Labs

Details of this Sligo based communications services company, with project experience in the areas of cable television, high speed (ATM) networks, wireless cable (MMDS), digital TV (QAM modulation) and market surveys
http://www.screen.ie/Business_connect/nwlabs/index.html

Northwest Radio

Contact and sales details for this local radio station broadcasting to Sligo, north Leitrim and south Donegal.
http://www.screen.ie/Business_connect/NW_Radio/index.html

Nova Northern Ireland Showcase

A host of information and useful links to Northern Ireland related pages. Nova's Marketplace Business Directory and Business Classifieds help you rapidly find export and service companies. There is also information about Northern Ireland with demographics and statistics, WorldShop Ireland, an Internet department store selling Irish products and works by leading artists, the Virtual Visit and a What's On guide.
http://www.iol.ie/~nova/nova1/pages/showcase.htm
Email: nova @ iol.ie

On s'Amuse Toy Shop

The world's first Virtual Wooden Toyshop — and it's in Dublin. A unique site, both virtually and physically. Their pages give a flavour of the the kinds of toys and games available in their store or by mail, plus an opportunity to play many games and link to interesting sites elsewhere on the Internet such as the chess problem of the month and much more.
http://www.internet-eireann.ie/toyshop/
Email: onsamuse@internet-eireann.ie
(Françoise & Don McBrien)

O'Neill Family History

Desmond O'Neill of Omeath has produced the most comprehensive unitary compilation of records relating to the O'Neill family of Ireland, garnered from a plethora of ancient and modern sources, with 538 pages, hand-written throughout in calligraphy script, adorned with 71 motifs or illustrations which include coats-of-arms, flags, escutcheons, portraits and maps. Only 500 numbered and signed copies of this book are available for sale world-wide at a cost of IR£3000, including packaging, shipping, and insurance.
http://www.ireland.net/marketplace/oneill/
Email: oneill@ieunet.ie

Please email changes or new URLs to mnugent@internet-eireann.ie or mnugent@iol.ie
Please also email me if you have difficulty locating a page, and I will try to assist you.

Private Eye — http://www.intervid.co.uk/intervid/eye/gateway.html | The URL File

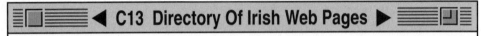

O'Mara Motors
The main distributor for Toyota vehicles in the Limerick area, their page includes information on the company, employees, the Toyota range of vehicles, the O'Mara stock of used vehicles, plus details on hiring a car and information on the Limerick area.
http://www.iol.ie/~omara/omm/omm_0.html

O'Reilly, Ferris, MIAVI
Details of properties on offer from this Kildare based auctioneer, including various residential properties plus (at time of writing) Riverside Stud, Teascon.
http://www.ireland.net/marketplace/ homehunters/oreilly/
Email: oreilly@property.ie

Original Print Gallery
This Temple Bar, Dublin business specialises in handmade limited edition prints — etchings, lithographs, woodcuts and silk screens — representing the work of a wide selection of the best of Irish and international artists both emerging and established. Their Web page includes both illustrations and artists statements.
http://www.internet-eireann.ie/Adnet/clients/ print/html/gallery.htm

---

PaddyNet
Absolutely loads of Irish-related information. Links include Fógra (the noticeboard), virtual blarney, The Island (mythology, folklore, history, literature, placenames, ancient sites), a green pages directory of Irish Web pages, PaddyNet post office, Creation (music, art, writing, fashion, fil, architecture), and The Craic (sport, blarney, religion and more).
http://www.paddynet.ie/
E-mail: info@webfactory.ie

Paddy Waldron's Home Page
When not lecturing in Economics at Trinity College Dublin, Paddy Waldron maintains four very interesting Irish Web pages — Paddy's Genealogy Page, Paddy Waldron's Bookmarks, the Virtual Tourist Guide to Ireland and What's New on the Web in Ireland. His home page will give you some more information on the man himself and what else he has done in the real world.
http://www.bess.tcd.ie/pwaldron.htm
Email: pwaldron@tcd.ie

Pettigrew Interior Plants
One of Irelands largest Interior Landscaping Contractors. You can download an Interactive multimedia catalogue, request a quotation or send your comments, visit The Stanley Pettigrew Exhibition of Paintings or follow links to a wealth of plant information.
http://www.internet-eireann.ie/pettigrew/ petplant.htm
Email: mpettigr@iol.ie

Pettigrew, Stanley, Exhibition
An online exhibition of oil paintings by one of Ireland's foremost landscape painters. All paintings are 20" x 30" oils on canvas and can be purchased directly from the artist.
http://www.iol.ie/resource/pettigrew/ petpla5.htm
Email: mpettigr@iol.ie

PFH Computer Systems
Deatils on the largest reseller of computers in the Munster area. Links to information on the company's main areas of operations — sales, training, support and maintenance, contract personnel, programming services and Internet services.
http://www.iol.ie/resource/pfh/
Email: pfhcomp@iol.ie

Phoenix Park Woodland Conservation Project
Anyone with Irish lineage can now plant some new roots in the Emerald Isle, without lifting a shovel or setting foot on Irish soil. For $40, you can have trees planted at Dublin's Phoenix Park in your own name or in the names of your ancestors. This service is part of a Rehab Foundation national reforestation program in Ireland.
http://ireland.iol.ie/resource/imi/rehab/

Piercom
Will your software handle the roll-over into the year 2000 correctly? Piercom offers services

---

Note: As the Web is continually evolving, some of these pages may have moved or expired. Ask for details at the email address — if listed — which is less likely to have changed.

| The URL File | **Psyche Journal — http://hcrl.open.ac.uk/psyche/psyche** |

and technolgies for software re-engineering, reverse engineering and re-documentation, plus services for documenting and scoping Year 2000 problems in Legacy applications.
http://www.commerce.ie/cp/piercom/
Email: smithc@ul.ie

Political Documents

❑ The full text of the Irish Constitution is at *http://www.maths.tcd.ie/pub/Constitution/index.html*

❑ The February 1995 Agreed Framework Document on Northern Ireland is at *http://jfd.compapp.dcu.ie/jfd.html*

❑ The December 1993 Joint Declaration on Northern Ireland is at *http://www.bess.tcd.ie/dclrtn.htm*

❑ The text of the Maastricht Treaty is at *gopher://fatty.law.cornell.edu:70/11/foreign/maastricht*

❑ The 1995 Irish Government Green Paper on Broadcasting is at *http://wwwavc.ucd.ie/broadcasting*

Poolbeg Press
Information and online ordering for Poolbeg books from Patricia Scanlon, Maeve Binchy, Anne Schulman, children's books, poetry, a little something else plus miscellanous titles.
http://www.iol.ie/resource/imi/irishmall/poolbeg/
Email: poolbeg@iol.ie

PostGEM
This electronic communications subsidiary of An Post was established to provide cost-effective, electronically based communications solutions for businesses. The Web page includes links to information on PostGEM services. Through a strategic alliance with Ireland OnLine, they have increased the local access options available to Irish Internet users.
http://www.iol.ie/postgem/
gilld@postgem.infonet.com

Premier Banking & Direct Insurance
Subsidiary companies of Bank Of Ireland.

Premier Banking offers personal loans exclusively by telephone to people who earn more than £12,000 per annum. The page includes a calculator where you type in an amount you might want to borrow and over how long you want to repay it, and it will tell what the monthly repayments would be. Premier Direct Insurance Services offers private motor car insurance to Irish motorists.
http://www.iol.ie/premier/

Premier Cycling Holidays
A Web brochure detailing the tours and facilities available from Premier Cycling Holidays, which is based near Portumna and whose tours are designed to take you through up to seven counties at your own pace.
http://www.iol.ie/~nbs/premier.htm

Queen's University Belfast
Very comprehensive site with details on academic schools and departments, academic services, administration, clubs, societies and associations, computing services, general information, industrial services, library Services, special interest groups at Queen's. Also includes links to other information sources such as a local entertainment guide, locations requested by students, national UK services and sources outside Queen's.
http://www.qub.ac.uk/
Email: R.Gregg@qub.ac.uk

Radioactive 95.5 FM
A radio station which operates on a collective basis and whose volunteer prsenters broadcast illegally to the greater Dublin area seven days a week. Its shows include Radio Net Ireland, an Internet information programme.
http://www.internet-eireann.ie/Dojo/radioact/radioact.htm
Email: active@dojo.internet-eireann.ie.

Please email changes or new URLs to mnugent@internet-eireann.ie or mnugent@iol.ie
Please also email me if you have difficulty locating a page, and I will try to assist you.

Quilting — http://ttsw.com/MainQuiltingPage.html | The URL File

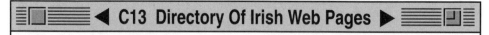

Radio Caroline Dublin

No connection with the original Radio Caroline that broadcast from the 1960s through to the 1990s, Radio Caroline Dublin is an illegal radio station that can be heard on 102.5 Mhz FM. Their Web page includes an index of legal and "free" radio station frequencies in the Dublin area.

http://www.internet-eireann.ie/Dojo/caroline/
caroline.htm
Email: caroline@dojo.internet-eireann.ie

Raidió na Gaeltachta

Information and some audio files from Raidió na Gaeltachta, which broadcasts to between 85,000 and 130,000 listeners all over Ireland on various bands from 92 to 94FM and also on 102.7FM.

http://wombatix.iol.ie/rnag/
Email: micheal@www.wombat.ie

Rand McNally Media Services

This Shannon based company offers diverse technologies ranging from automated airline tickets to digital mapping, computerised truck routing and high speed childerns book binding. Page includes an online feedback form for requesting further information.

http://www.randmedia.ie/rand/

Rathe House

Rathe House is an Irish Equestrian Centre nestling in over one thousand acres in County Meath. Its Web page outlines a typical stay at the house — guest accommodation is in the Coach House, converted to accommodate parties of up to 10 people, and the equestrian activities are followed by an evening of traditional Irish dancing and entertainment.

http://www.ripi.ie/ipi/rathe/

Read Ireland Bookstore

An online catalogue for the first Internet bookstore dedicated to Irish books. Huge collection of books in thirty five categories ranging alphabetically from antiques to tourist guides. There is also an online search facility for you to look for the exact book you want.

http://www.internet-eireann.ie/Readireland/
Email: readireland@internet-eireann.ie

Readout Instrumentation Signpost

Readout is the only journal of Instrumentation and Control produced in Ireland. Circulation is restricted to some 2000 users, teachers and vendors in the instrumentation world in Ireland. The readout page includes links to the Internet Directory of Instrumentation, a world wide directory launched in 1995, information on exhibitions and conferences throughout the world and several important Web resources on standards.

http://www.iol.ie/~readout/index.html
Email: readout@iol.ie (Eoin O'Riain)

Reddington & Associates

This Mayo based business runs training courses to help companies to gain an in-depth understanding of ISO Series of Standards to lead an audit effectively. Their Web page includes links to details on course objectives, who should attend the course, programme details, course leaders and details of FÁS grants available to Irish companies for this course.

http://www.internet-eireann.ie/insight/quality/
index.html
Email: quality@insight.ie (Martin Reddington)

Reflex Magnetics

This Waterford based company, which provides computer security, anti-virus and PC software management products, is an Irish agent for disknet, ThunderBYTE and VET Anti-Virus software. Their Web page includes links to a products page, a file transfer menu and a Web-store.

http://www.iol.ie/~ralf/welcome.html
Email: ralf@iol.ie

Reviews From The Forbidden Planet

Fairly self-explanatory, really. Reviews of comics supplied by the Forbidden Planet on Dublin's Dawson Street. Comprehensive set of links.

http://www.maths.tcd.ie/mmm/
ReviewsFromTheForbiddenPlanet.html

Rodine Software Systems

Details of software services provided by this Waterford based firm, including a solicitors management accounting system, an

Note: As the Web is continually evolving, some of these pages may have moved or expired. Ask for details at the email address — if listed — which is less likely to have changed.

The URL File	Quote Generator — http://www.ugcs.caltech.edu/~werdna/fun.html

accountants time recording and management accounting system and a property database and accounting systemfor auctioneers.
http://www.iol.ie/~rodine/
Email: rodine@iol.ie

Rogers, Terry, Bookmakers
Regulary updated betting odds and results on the British premier soccer league, American football, the Smurfit European Open and Irish and English Horse Racing Results.
http://www.internet-eireann.ie/i-events/
rogers/tr1.html
Email: trogers@internet-eireann.ie

Rooney Autioneers
Accommodation particulars plus interior and exterior photos of houses on sale through this Galway based Auctioneer firm, along with details of other professional services offered in the fields of property acquisitions, rent reviews, valuations, investments and finance.
http://www.infopoint.ie/rooney/rooney.html

Rosgraerin House
Details of facilities and costs for staying at Rosgraerin House, Dunshaughlin, County Meath, plus links to information on local places of interest such as The Hill of Tara, and the megalithic tombs of Newgrange, Knowth, and Dowth.
http://www.internet-eireann.ie/ipi/guest/
rosgraer/index.html
Email:rosgraerin@internet-eireann.ie

Ross, Edmund Studios
Details of services offered by this Dublin based studio, which specialises in a number of arts, including the refurbishment and restoration of old photographs by hand, wedding photography, studio portraiture and commercial and industrial photography.
http://www.iol.ie/~adamski/eds.htm
Email: adamski@iol.ie

Royal Auctioneers
Links to details of properties on sale from Royal Auctioneers, mainly in the County Meath area.
http://www.ireland.net/marketplace/
homehunters/royal/
Email: royal@property.ie

RTCnet
The RTCnet is a network which is currently being commissioned to connect all of the Regional Technical Colleges in Ireland. Digital leased lines have been commissioned to each of the connected sites and two network connection points have been established at Athlone and Cork. The entire network is linked to the HEAnet at Dublin. The site includes links to pages on the RTCs at Athlone, Carlow, Cork, Dundalk, Galway, Letterkenny, Limerick, Sligo, Tallaght and Waterford. They are maintained by the Projects Group at UCD including Alan Byrne, Louis Twomey, Brian Donovan, Paul Ryan, and Andrew Darby.
http://www.ucd.ie/projects_group/rtcnet.html

RTE To Everywhere Home Page
Morning Ireland On The Internet! An experimental project to assess the viability of making small segments of RTE news broadcasts available on the Internet in the form of digital sound files. About a week's news headlines are kept on-line. These are very large files (480KB per minute of air time) so please think about the bandwidth implications and about those trying to do real work on the host machines before selecting one.
http://www.bess.tcd.ie/ireland/rte.htm
Email: pmurphy@nrao.edu

Sabhal Mór Ostaig
The home page of this Gaelic speaking college on the Isle of Skye includes links to Fiosrachadh mun Cholaiste, Fiosrachadh mun Ghàidhlig, Ceanglaichean gu fiosrachadh air an t-Saoghal Mhór, agus an t-Eilean Sitheanach agus áiteachan timcheall air. There is also a link to an English language version of the page.
http://www.smo.uhi.ac.uk/

St Patrick's College Maynooth
One of the colleges of the National University of Ireland, with almost 4,000 students on campus, Maynooth is situated 15 miles from Dublin. The home page includes links to details

---

Please email changes or new URLs to mnugent@internet-eireann.ie *or* mnugent@iol.ie
Please also email me if you have difficulty locating a page, and I will try to assist you.

---

of available courses in the faculties of Arts, Celtic Studies, Philosophy and Science, Web servers in the departments of Computer Science, Mathematics and Experimental Physics plus information about the college library and museum and the Maynooth Alumni Association.
http://www.may.ie/
Email: webmaster@ailm.may.ie

Sail West
Details and costs of sailing holidays from this Connemara based business, whose cruising range extends north along the coastline of County Mayo or south as far as the Blasket Islands off the end of the Dingle peninsula in West Kerry.
http://www.internet-eireann.ie/Ireland/sailw1.html

Saris
As well as providing straps to the backpacker market, Saris has now moved into the development of Web presentations on the Internet for hostels, transport companies, and activity operators in New Zealand using old ties and relationships. Based in Cork and Auckland, Saris is also developing an online Backpacker Guide for Net users.
http://www.iol.ie/~saris/about.html
Email: saris@iol.ie

Screengate
See Ireland America Web entry.

Screenphones
See NorthWest Connect entry.

SelfGrow Ltd
A Tullamore based company set up in March 1995 to provide basic computer literacy courses for the Midlands area of Ireland.
http://www.internet-eireann.ie/SelfGrow/default.htm

Shamrock Rovers (unofficial page)
Page for people who prefer watching a bottom-of-the-table team of footballing nomads instead of Bohemians. Links to match fixtures, results and reports plus all sorts of information on Rovers and its players.
http://paul.maths.may.ie:8000/Rovers.html

Shannon Development
An integrated development agency responsible for job creation in the Shannon area including through air traffic promotion at Shannon Airport, the Shannon Free Zone, tourism, rural development and indigenous industry in the Shannon Region, and management and development of the National Technological Park at Plassey. Page includes links to details on industry, equity, property, what's new and background.
http://www.commerce.ie/shannon-dev/
Email: kingj@shannon-dev.ie

Sheepwalk House
Services, directions, prices and booking information for staying at this Wexford holiday accomodation, approved by Family Homes of Ireland.
http://www.eire.com/turas/Sheepwalk/index.html
Email: web@eire.com

Sherry & Associates
Auctioneers, Estate Agents and Valuers, the practice is involved in all areas of property sales, from residential to commercial, agricultural holdings and estates to investment properties and second homes. Their Web page includes details of a selection of properties which they are currently marketing, together with photographs.
http://www.internet-eireann.ie/ipi/sherry/

Sinead O'Connor (unofficial page)
Maintained by Sinead fan Jeff Russell in Washington, this page includes links to a discography, lyrics of Sinead's singles and duets, a biography, quotes, essays, poems, interviews, pictures and other Sinead links.
http://www.engr.ukans.edu/~jrussell/music/sinead/sinead.html
Email: jrussell@washington.engr.ukans.edu

Sinn Féin (unofficial page)
Maintained by Brian McKinley in Colorado Springs, USA, this unofficial (as opposed to either Official or Provisional, but very much more Provisional than Official) Sinn Féin page includes a very comprehensive collection of information on Sinn Féin including summaries of articles in An Phoblacht, various interviews

---

Note: As the Web is continually evolving, some of these pages may have moved or expired. Ask for details at the email address — if listed — which is less likely to have changed.

| The URL File | Random Quotes — http://alpha.acast.nova.edu/quotes.html |

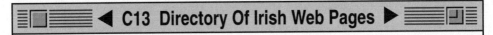
with leading Sinn Fein figures, IRA statements and interviews and more.
http://www.rmii.com/mckinley/sinnfein.html
Email: mckinley@rmii.com

Sligo RTC

Pages under development in August of 1995 included links to pages with details on management and school structure, admissions office, computer department, School of Business & Humanities, School of Science and School of Engineering. See also RTCnet entry.
http://ns.rtc-Sligo.ie/
Email: cahilli@s4.rtc-sligo.ie (Ian Cahill)

Sligo Weekender

An Internet edition of this weekly local newspaper, launched on the Net in mid-September 1995, with local news and pictures and an index of back issues.
http://www.screen.ie/weekender/
Email: weekender@screen.ie

Software Computing Power

An Irish company which works in co-operation with Software AG Germany, their home page includes links to details on CICS, X/Open resource management, cross platform help and training services.
http://www.internet-eireann.ie/scp/index.htm
Email: info@scp.ie

Software Expressions

Provide a consultancy service to organisations and firms who wish to get started on the Internet, and a publishing service for those who wish to make information available on the Internet. Their Web page includes links to details on Irish job vacancies, Irish tourist facilities and Irish recruitment consultants and employment agencies
http://www.internet-eireann.ie/Ireland/swexp.html
Email: swexp@internet-eireann.ie

Software Innovations

Specialise in client–server applications, networking and database products. Their Web page includes a profile of the company, products and services plus links to a planned international marketplace directory for Irish products and services.

http://www.internet-eireann.ie/innovate/si_home.htm
Email: frankdaly@internet-eireann.ie

Sothern Auctioneers

Links to details of properties on sale from Sothern Auctioneers, mainly in the Carlow, Waterford, Kildare and Wicklow areas.
http://www.ireland.net/marketplace/homehunters/soth/
Email: soth@property.ie

South of Ireland Language Centre

This Cork based language centre was established in 1969. On its home page, a brief explanation of the various aspects of the centre is given under the following headings — goals of the organisation, courses, teaching staff, classes and their summer school at which inspectors are invited from Trinity College, London to evaluate those students who wish to sit for the Trinity College, London external examinations.
http://www.cis.ie/marketplace/silc/
Email: cormacl@easylink.cis.ie
(Dr Cormac Lankford)

Southeast Technical Services

Located in Kilkenny and run by John Reid, STS works in electronics and software development and information services for companies wishing to maintain a head start on new technology at the lowest possible cost.
http://www.iol.ie/~jreid/sts/index.html
Email: jreid@iol.ie

Space Technology Ireland

STI has worked on space science missions mounted by ESA, NASA, Russia and Japan. They now also apply their design and engineering methods, developed initally for space applications, to problem solving and product development in a wide variety of ground based industries including electronics and software design, optimisation of system design parameters, custom built fault tolerant data processing systems, stress, strain and thermal analysis and applications of laser technology in medical diagnosis and environmental monitoring.
http://www.internet-eireann.ie/stil/
E-Mail: stil@may.ie

Please email changes or new URLs to mnugent@internet-eireann.ie *or* mnugent@iol.ie
Please also email me if you have difficulty locating a page, and I will try to assist you.

Roleplaying Resources — http://www.cqs.washington.edu/~surge/rpg.html | The URL File

SpeechWriters

Speeches written for all social, business and sporting occasions and emailed straight to you, either personalised or pre-prepared wedding speeches for everyone from the groom to the clergyman.
http://www.iol.ie/resource/imi/irishmall/speech/
Email: speechwriters@iol.ie

Standun

Browse and purchase directly from this Connemara based family drapery store, highly recommended by Foder's, Fielding, Frommers, TWA & Routard travel guides. Their page includes links to on-line shopping, a travel guide to Connemara and times past.
http://www.interact.ie/marketplace/interact/standun/index.html
Email: standun@iol.ie

Summerhill House

Details of facilities and costs for staying at Summerhill House, Wexford, plus information on local amenities.
http://www.eire.com/turas/Summerhill/index.html
Email: web@eire.com

Tallaght RTC
See RTCnet entry.

Tara Cruisers
Shannon Holidays

Based in Carrick-on-Shannon, Co. Leitrim, Tara provides luxury cruiser hire on the River Shannon. The page includes links to details on the Shannon, the company, the boats, agents, price list, booking form and getting there.
http://www.iol.ie/resource/imi/tara/
Email: tarac@iol.ie

Tasc Software Developers

Specialists in agri-busines software solutions such as breed management programmes for breeders of all types of animals, their Web page includes a comprehensive set of links to information on services offered.

http://www.internet-eireann.ie/tasc/
Email: brendon@internet-eireann.ie

Technical Resource Consultants

Links from this page include an introduction to the company, a list of their most popular Windows training courses, plus their design and bureau services, consultancy services and support services.
http://ireland.iol.ie/%7Etrc/
Email: trc@iol.ie

Technosoft

Web page of this Terenure based business includes links to online technical support (multi-vendor hardware and software), discussion newsgroups plus software archives, helper applications and file services.
http://www.iol.ie/~techsoft/
Email: info@technosoft.iol.ie

Telecom Eireann

The TE Web page includes a link to the online Telecom Eireann Museum of Communications, which includes a history of Irish tele-communications, plus information on the museum function, staff and heritage collection.
http://www.hq2.telecom.ie/
Email: postmaster@telecom.ie

Teltec Ireland

Based in Dublin City University, Teltec Ireland represents a partnership between third-level institutions and industry, established by the Irish government to provide research and development services in telecommunications. Links include information on intelligent networks, video coding, hardware design and broadband networks.
http://www.teltec.dcu.ie/
Email: webmaster@www.teltec.dcu.ie

Tetrix Engineering

Serves industrial companies in the technical and non-technical sector by supplying custom-solutions to problems in the areas of services (including design and provision of Web pages), software development (Windows based software in all technical areas to customer requirements) and electronics (design, manufacturing and prototyping). Tetrix designs and manufactures its products to individual

---

Note: As the Web is continually evolving, some of these pages may have moved or expired. Ask for details at the email address — if listed — which is less likely to have changed.

| The URL File | **The Roswell Centre — http://www.atlas.co.uk/paragon/roswell.html** |

customer requirements and specifications.
http://www.internet-eireann.ie/tetrix/
Email: johannes@tetrix.internet-eireann.ie

The End On The Net
The online resource of RTE's Friday and Saturday late night (11pm to 1am) television show with Barry Murphy, Sean Moncrieff and specialist guests who provide you with some unusual examples of life on this planet. An infectious puppet called Sceptic makes the odd indiscreet contribution. Saturday night also features weekly contributions from the Internet and viewers email which is what this Web site is all about. At time of wriing, included links to The End Internet Novel, your suggestions for next season and Email Funnies.
http://www.iol.ie/resource/theend/
Email: theend@iol.ie

Thesaurus Software Ltd
A company formed in 1991 by Paul Byrne and Tom Horan, the initial project undertaken was the production of payroll software for the Irish market. Shortly afterwards a Timesheet Project was under taken. Details on both projects are available on their Web page.
http://www.internet-eireann.ie/proll/

Thin Lizzy (unofficial page)
A page created by American Lizzy fan Ed Poole to commemorate the artistic life of Philip Lynott and preserve the memory of Thin Lizzy. Includes links to Thin Lizzy archives (lyrics, pictures and text), history, timeline, organizations and much more.
http://www2.uncg.edu/~edpoole/
Email: edpoole@turing.uncg.edu

Tourism & Travel
The Ireland Online Tourism Index includes links to pages with information on foreign holiday and travel information, Tara Cruisers Shannon Holidays, fishing, visiting the Aran Island with Aer Arann, Wombat Research's Complete Guide to Galway, Greenane Riding Centre, holiday apartments in Connemara and Bruckless House accommodation in Co. Donegal.
http://www.iol.ie/resource/tourism/tourism.html
Email: WebMaster@iol.ie

Tralee RTC
A very comprehensive set of pages on Tralee Regional Technical College, including links to pages on college structure, administration, schools and courses, senior academic and administrative job vacancies in Tralee RTC, college floor plans, the Industrial Liaison Office, the Kerry Innovation Centre, contact points for any staff member, student participation in the Erasmus programme, the Kerry International Summer School '95, train and bus services to Tralee and much more.
http://ns.rtc-tralee.ie/traleeRTChp.html
Email: lillis@bosheasrv0.rtc-tralee.ie (Deirdre Lillis) or paulc@staffmail.rtc-tralee.ie (Paul Collins)

Trident Holiday Homes
Details of facilities and costs for staying at Trident Holiday Homes in Dublin, Galway, Waterford, Clare, Kerry and Mayo.
http://www.internet-eireann.ie/Ireland/trident.html

Trinity College Dublin
Founded in 1592, Trinity College is the oldest university in Ireland. It also has one of the best and most up-to-date Web sites in Ireland. Includes links to pages on TCD history, maps, pictures, visitor information, academic structure, research activites of academics and research units located on campus, research papers available on College servers, postgraduate research opportunities, a course directory, library and information services, other College services and facilities and a guide for the College community using the Internet.
http://www.tcd.ie/
Email: secretary@tcd.ie

U2 (unofficial pages)
The Yahoo directory page of links to U2 pages on the Net. Too many entries to list here; well worth checking it out yourself.
http://www.yahoo.com/Entertainment/Music/Artists/U2/

Please email changes or new URLs to mnugent@internet-eireann.ie or mnugent@iol.ie
Please also email me if you have difficulty locating a page, and I will try to assist you.

Royal Society of Chemistry — http://chemistry.rsc.org/rsc/ | The URL File

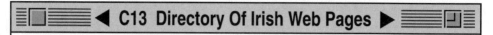

Ulster American Folk Park

An outdoor museum at Castletown, Co. Tyrone, designed to tell the story of the waves of emigrants who left Ulster for the New World in the eighteenth and nineteenth centuries and of the contribution they made to the USA throughout the whole period of its birth and development. The page includes links to a map of the park, an Emigrants Exhibition, a ship and dockside gallery page and news of new developments at the park.
http://www.ireland.net/marketplace/uafp/

Ulster Historical Foundation

A non-profit making organisation, founded in 1956 to promote Ulster history and genealogy, and to make information about the sources in this field more readily available. Links from this page include an introduction to the Ulster Historical Foundation, a comprehensive list of books published by the foundation which can be purchased by mail order, publications by Familia (the Belfast Family History and Cultural Heritage Centre), the Irish ancestor conference "Famine Forebears", and contact addresses.
http://www.ireland.net/marketplace/uhf/

Ulster Unionist Party

Policy and aims of the Ulster Unionist Party under leader David Trimble, plus links to current affairs from a unionist perspective and a visitors book to add your own thoughts.
http://www.gpl.net/customers/uup/
Email: webmaster@www.gpl.net

Ulysses

An excellent and visually attractive Irish business and leisure guide, Ulysses is also home to the Virtual Irish Pub (see separate listing). The Ulysses home page includes links to tourism, hotel, hostel and B&B guides based on a "clickable" map of Ireland. It also has evolving entertainment and business sections, and of course the Virtual Irish Pub (VIP).
http://www.misty.com/ulysses/
Email: ulysses@visunet.ie

Underground Club

Ireland's first CyberCafé, now located at Crowe Street in Dublin and renamed Internet HQ. A private club where members can relax and enjoy a social environment free of alcohol abuse and smoke. Open from 18:00 until 06:00. Vegetarian food and finger snacks. Distractions: Theatre, Music, Jazz, Classical, Poetry, Lectures and Discussions, Daily Papers, Books, Art and Language Classes, Original Cinema and Video, Yoga, Hobbies, Internet Computer Access, TV and Board Games.
http://www.internet-eireann.ie/Underground/
Email: patnpat@underground.ie

Unibol

A Newtownabbey based software tools company providing migration solutions from IBM System platforms to open systems. Unibol products are available on all leading UNIX platforms.
http://www.unibol.com/
Email: unibol@unibol.com

Unit Instruments Ltd

Details of this Dublin company which manufactures mass flow technology equipment, analytical tools including mass flow controllers for controlling gases, mass flow meters and other products.
http://www.internet-eireann.ie/bdi/home/unit/index.html

University College Cork

Another very comprehensive university site, with academic information by faculty and department, including regulations, fees, appointments, major research projects, coming events, conference organisation and accommodation, the 150th anniversary celebrations, clubs and societies, student accommodation, and UCC's own Campus Radio Station. Closes with a thought for the day; August 22nd's was "Had this been an actual emergency, we would have fled in terror, and you would not have been informed".
http://www.ucc.ie/webentry.shtml

University College Dublin

UCD is the largest university institution in Ireland. Its student and staff numbers make it equivalent to a town the size of Athlone. This Web site includes general College information and some useful and interesting pointers to other sites, plus an aerial view of the campus,

---

Note: As the Web is continually evolving, some of these pages may have moved or expired. Ask for details at the email address — if listed — which is less likely to have changed.

The URL File	Running — http://sunsite.unc.edu:80/drears/running/running.html

an active map of campus information servers and the UCD Graduate School of Business Web site. Also includes links to UCD's Campus Wide Information Service, UCD Gopher, UCD Online Library Catalogue and UCD Telephone Book.
http://www.ucd.ie/
Email: webmaster@nova.ucd.ie

UCD Projects Group
This group was established in UCD at the start of 1993 to manage the growing number of externally funded projects being undertaken by Computing Services. The group is specifically tasked to take on strategically important projects for Computing Services such as National Research Networking and Advanced Applications research.
http://slarti.ucd.ie/projects_group.html
Email: support@slarti.ucd.ie

University College Galway
This site is maintained by the Management Information Services Web server at University College Galway. It includes an introduction to the UCG faculties (arts, Celtic studies, commerce, engineering, law, medicine, science) plus details on college enquiries, college officers, 150th anniversary celebrations (1845–1995), international summer schools and UCG graduate liaison Services.
http://www.mis.ucg.ie/
Email: t.oceallaigh@mis.ucg.ie

University College Galway (unofficial pages)
A Wombat Research site. Links to information on academic departments (so far mainly science, engineering, research and services), student information (including clubs and societies, Galway night clubs, banks, accommodation, Students Union and FLIRT FM Student Radio). Also includes links to information on the Manufacturing Research Centre and a UCG slide show.
http://wombatix.physics.ucg.ie/ucg/ucg.html
Email: www@wombatix.physics.ucg.ie.

University of Limerick Information Exchange

Includes links to University of Limerick general information, how to find people and places, publications, current events, visitor information, prospective students, academic departments, research centres, research activities and opportunities, University Administration, library and information services, accommodation, counselling, sports activities, entertainment and leisure. Also includes access information and services available on the Internet, the World Wide Web, and University of Limerick servers.
http://www.ul.ie/
Email: webeditor@ul.ie

University of Ulster
Covers four campuses at Belfast, Coleraine, Derry and Jordanstown. A very comprehensive site covering the history of the University, its campus structure, visitor information, shops, theatre, contact information, the academic and non-academic structures of the University, research information including opportunities for research study, library services, computing services, Unibooks (the University Bookshop), electronic information services, postgraduate and undergraduate courses, applying for a course prospectus, joint initiatives, projects and ventures with other Universities and Organisations, news and events, job vacancies and miscellaneous services.
http://dsets.ulst.ac.uk/
Email: www@ulst.ac.uk (Mike Diver)

VIP (the Virtual Irish Pub)
This is the Internet's authentic Irish pub, where you can go for some light entertainment and chat with whoever else happens to be there at the time. You just type in your contribution to the discussion, reload the page and see who has responded. All of the pub discussion areas have their equivalent mailing lists. The meeting place includes links to the main bar, the fancy lounge, the upstairs bar, the beer garden, the joke(r's) corner and the lovers' table. The Irish interest section has links to Irish questions and answers, a

---

Please email changes or new URLs to mnugent@internet-eireann.ie or mnugent@iol.ie
Please also email me if you have difficulty locating a page, and I will try to assist you.

genealogy forum, a history forum, a politics forum and a sports forum. There is also an emigrant's snug, and market place and job search links, plus an experimental version of live chat at the VIP. A site to put in your bookmark file.
http://www.misty.com/ulysses/vip/
Email: justin@visunet.ie (Justin Vincent)

Virtual Tourist Guide to Ireland
Another Paddy Waldron page. Includes links to pages about the four provinces of Ireland, Irish universities, tracing your Irish ancestors, the Irish language, Irish literature and theatre on the Web, Irish music on the Web, Irish economics, politics and current affairs, a page on Dublin and links to other Irish tourist guides on the Internet.
http://www.bess.tcd.ie/ireland.htm
Email: pwaldron@tcd.ie (Paddy Waldron)

Virtual Yachting
Information on the 1720, a yacht designed by Tony Castro Ltd, naval architects, at the request of a group of sailing enthusiasts who are members of the World's oldest yacht club, The Royal Cork founded in 1720.
http://www.aardvark.ie/1720/
rclancy@nmrc.ucc.ie

Visicon Irish Star Trek Convention 1996
The convention will be held in Dublin City University on June 22–23, 1996 in aid of the Coombe Maternity Hospital. While the main theme will be Trek related, there will be several related exhibits which attendees can visit throughout the 36 hour event.
http://www.internet-eireann.ie/Visicon/visicon.htm
Email: gnugent@internet-eireann.ie

V. Grafix
Creators of the Ulysses and Virtual Irish Pub Web pages, Visual Graphics Artwork, offers services in the areas of artwork origination and localisation, photo editing, HTML authoring and Web server set-up.
Email: ulysses@vgrafix.internet-eireann.ie

Voyager Technologies Ireland
An international company with Dublin offices which specialises in developing Windows software for the travel and credit card industries. Page includes information on VTI around the world, and the VTI-Link development environment.
http://www.iol.ie/~markl/vti.htm
Email: markl@iol.ie

W3 Services
An Internet marketing services and consultancy company based in the Limerick Innovation centre, specialising in the integration of Internet communication methods and business practices.
http://www.w3s.ie/w3s/
Email: info@w3s.ie

Waterford City
This site is maintained at Waterford RTC by the W4 Group (Waterford World Wide Web). It includes a brief history of Waterford, an Arts and Entertainments page, a news desk with local, national and international news, the Waterford Images Gallery, accomodation in Waterford, aspects of Irish culture and links to some other interesting Web sites.
http://centris.rtc-waterford.ie/
Email: w3master@mips.rtc-waterford.ie

Waterford RTC
See RTCnet entry.

Watermarque
Information on services provided including sales promotion, direct marketing, public relations, brand publicity, brand advertising, sponsorship negotiation and management.
http://www.iol.ie/~wmarque/
Email: wmarque@iol.ie

The Web Factory
Creators of the PaddyNet Web pages, The Web Factory offers services in the areas of Internet marketing and PR, graphic design and copywriting, HTML coding, programmed applications, Internet training and Web site storage and maintenance.
http://www.webfactory.ie/
Email: info@webfactory.ie

Note: As the Web is continually evolving, some of these pages may have moved or expired. Ask for details at the email address — if listed — which is less likely to have changed.

The URL File	Scottish National Party — http://www.tardis.ed.ac.uk/~alba/snp/

What's New on the Web in Ireland
One of the very useful sites maintained by Paddy Waldron at TCD, this page is modelled on the What's New With NCSA Mosaic page at the University of Illinois. To give a flavour of what you will find, links at time of writing included the Irish American Partnership, ERA-Maptec maps and satellite photos, the Original Print Gallery, Temple Bar, Knicker Box Swimwear '95, Cleo Ireland, AMEV Insurance, the National Theatre, the 6:30pm news from RTÉ Radio 1, the Four Provinces page and the Standun online catalogue.
http://www.bess.tcd.ie/newinirl.htm
Email: *pwaldron@tcd.ie (Paddy Waldron)*

Winc
Details of Web design and consultancy services available from the creators of the Web pages for Iona Technologies, Electronic Frontier Ireland and the European Researchers Network.
http://www.winc.ie/
Email: *info@winc.ie*

Wizsigns
Cavan based company which supplies scenic views of Ireland printed in full colour on Irish made t-shirts, sweat-shirts etc. Page includes sample photos and an online order form, or you can if you wish send your own photographs and have them printed on the shirt.
http://www.iol.ie/~wizsigns/t_shirts.htm
Email: *wizsigns@.iol.ie*

Wombat Research Guide to Galway
Wombat Research is a non-profit, all-for-fun organisation whose main projects are The Galway Guide and IRLNET (a database of Ireland related online resources). Active members are Joe Desbonnet (founder), Aoife Hegarty, Eoin Carroll and Dave Rynne. The Galway Guide includes links to Galway for beginners, backpackers guide to Galway, summer festivals, Galway Arts Festival, tourist information (maps, Aran Islands, tours), history of Galway. Also sections on shopping, eating, cafés, pubs, cinemas, theatre, live music, night clubs, new experimental food guide, transport and accommodation and local economy and commerce.
http://wombatix.physics.ucg.ie/galway/index.html
Email: *www@wombatix.physics.ucg.ie.*

Woodwards Auctioneers
Links to details of properties on sale from this Cork based auctioneering firm, including residential and commercial properties for sale, plus antique, fine art and silver auctions. There is also a home-match service where you can list your requirements.
http://www.eirenet.net/cork/woodwards/woodmail.htm
Email: *woodward@eirenet.net*

World Wide Stage
The aim of this page is to feature some of the best wriiters on the Internet today. Each day, authors, playwrights and poets present their work on the stage for your enjoyment. Includes today's features on the World Wide Stage, the latest additions to the collection and biographies of the authors whose work is featured.
http://www.iol.ie/~westrock/
Email: *westrock@iol.ie (Derek Doran)*

Wysiwyg
Based in Galway, Wysiwyg (what you see is what you get) have published two easy-to-follow and affordable guides for computer users: The Essential PageMaker 5 and The Essential PageMaker for the Macintosh. They also provide Web authoring, training and dtp services.
http://www.iol.ie/~wysiwyg/
Email: *wysiwyg@iol.ie*

Zandar Technologies
An Irish research & development company specialising in multi-image video equipment, whose products allow Cable/TV broadcasters to display various multi-image arrays of the TV channels being broadcast.
http://www.iol.ie/~zandar/
Email: *zandar@iol.ie*

Please email changes or new URLs to mnugent@internet-eireann.ie *or* mnugent@iol.ie
Please also email me if you have difficulty locating a page, and I will try to assist you.

Shaolin Martial Arts — http://www.webcom.com/~shaolin/ | The URL File

What you can do with partial access

← B14
Deciding
to get
online

← C11
So how
does it all
work?

Partial (or limited, or indirect) access to the Internet will allow you to use some, but not all, of the facilities available on the Internet. Exactly what you can or can't use will depend on the company with which you have your access account.

You will certainly be able to use email and most probably the Usenet newsgroups. You will not be able to directly log into other computers, or directly transfer files from other computers onto your own computer, or access World Wide Web pages. You will be able to do some of these things indirectly.

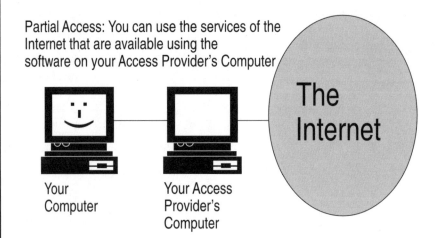

Partial Access: You can use the services of the Internet that are available using the software on your Access Provider's Computer

The Internet

Your Computer

Your Access Provider's Computer

Where you can get it

You can get an online account with a commercial computer network that provides its own services, which are entirely independent of the Internet. The biggest examples include America Online, CompuServe etc. Networks like these can also offer partial Internet access, as part of their overall service. Some also provide full Internet access. The important point to note is that, with partial Internet access, you can only use the sevices of the Internet that you can reach using the software on your Access Provider's computer.

The URL File | **Shareware Library — http://audrey.fagg.uni-lj.si/cgi.bin/shase/Form**

What you can do with full access

←B14
Deciding to get online

←C11
So how does it all work?

Full (or unlimited, or direct) access to the Internet will allow you to use any Internet facilities that you can reach using the software on your own computer. With full access, you can also have your own personal Internet domain address.

As well as being able to do more things, you can also do them simultaneously. For example, you can have one window open on your computer which is downloading a file from a computer in Canada, and another window open which is searching for information on a database in a computer in London.

Full Access: You can use the services of the Internet that are available using the software on your own Computer

Your Computer

Connection (either via

a message router or Your Access Provider's Computer)

The Internet

SLIP, PPP and other letters of the alphabet

To be able to use full access using a modem, you need either SLIP or PPP software on your computer. These are different protocols that allow your computer to behave as if it were directly attached to the Internet. In effect, while you are using either SLIP or PPP, your computer becomes part of the Internet, with its own unique Internet domain address.

In case it ever comes up as the final question in an important pub quiz, SLIP stands for Serial Line Internet Protocol, and PPP stands for Point-to-Point Protocol.

Shortwave Radio Catalogue — http://itre.unsecs.edu/radio/

The URL File

What you can do with dial-up access

← B14
Deciding to get online

← C11
So how does it all work?

Quick review: Partial (or limited, or indirect) access will allow you to use some of the facilities available on the Internet. Full (or unlimited, or direct) access will allow you to use whatever you can reach using the software on your own computer.

You can get either of these types of Internet access through a dial-up telephone account with an Internet Service Provider. Your computer telephones your Provider's computer, using a modem. While you keep the call open, your computer is linked either to your Provider's computer or directly to the Internet.

Dial-up Access: Your Computer telephones your Access Provider's Computer using a modem

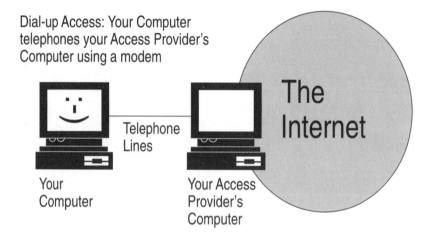

Telephone
Lines

The
Internet

Your
Computer

Your Access
Provider's
Computer

How much does it cost?

Typically, you pay your Access Provider a once-off connection fee (which can be as little as £15 for a single machine) plus an ongoing account fee (which can be as little as £10 a month for a single machine). Some Providers charge a set monthly fee, others charge you depending on how much time you spend on line.

All of this being part of the real world, you also pay Telecom Eireann for your phone bills. However, your only phone charges are for calls to your Provider. This means you can contact computers worldwide for the price of a local phone call.

| The URL File | **The Simpsons — http://www.digimark.net/TheSimpsons/** |

A permanent part of the Internet

Dedicated (or permanent) Internet access means that your computer, or more likely your local network, is permanently part of the Internet. You lease a line (e.g. from Telecom Eireann) connecting your network to your Access Provider. You also need a router (or message director) through which the flow of data between your network and that of your Provider is directed.

←B14
Deciding to get online

←C11
So how does it all work?

You can also have the equivalent of permanent access by having a specific modem and a specific phone line at your Access Provider dedicated to your own use.

Dedicated Access: Your computer or computer network is permanently part of the Internet

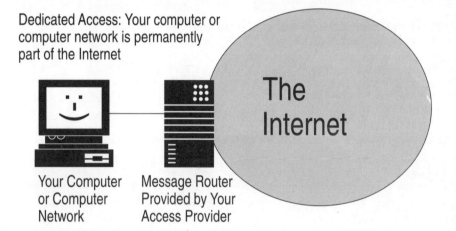

The Internet

Your Computer or Computer Network

Message Router Provided by Your Access Provider

How much does it cost?

A dedicated Internet link will cost you, at a minimum, several thousand pounds a year. It is unlikely to be economically viable unless you are a large institution or business, a government agency, or an independently wealthy individual with loads of time and nothing to do other than use the Internet.

If you are connecting a network of computers to the Internet, you can calculate whether a dedicated link or a dial-up link would be more or less expensive by comparing the costs of each with the amount of time your employees will spend on line.

Skepticism — http://wheel.ucdavis.edu/~btcarrol/skeptic/dictcont.html | The URL File

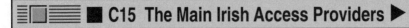
What to ask before getting an account

What services are provided? Email only or full access? Is that what you need?
How much does it cost? Is it a flat rate or are you charged by the time you spend online?
Can you connect to your Provider's system with a local phone call?
What computer and software do you have? Does the Provider supply software?
What modem do you have? Does the Service Provider support that type of modem?
What plans has the Provider to expand its resources as the number of subscribers grows?
What type of technical assistance and telephone support is provided?

← B15
Who provides access?

← C11
So how does it all work?

Indirect Access to the Internet in Ireland

You can get indirect access to the Internet by getting an account with a commercial online service. These services provide their own online information databases and discussion forums, along with a gateway to some or all of the facilities of the Internet.

Apple's eWorld	Price US$9.95 + VAT per hour online, converted into IR£. Further info: Freephone 1800 626096
Compu-Serve	Price US$12 for first 2 hours online per month, then 16 cents per minute. Further info: 0044 1272 760681
Microsoft Network	Hourly prices start at US$4.95 + VAT for the first three hours online, with a scale of charges for additional hours. Further info: Microsoft Sales. Tel: (01) 4502113

IEunet

IEunet is based in Dublin. It is the Irish partner in Eunet, a Europe-wide network. It offers full access to the Internet and other related Internet services and — through joint ventures with other companies — it is also part of *Cork Internet Services* and *Shannon Internet Services*.

← B15
Who provides access?

← C11
So how does it all work?

Services offered and Costs (Oct 1995) Contact IEunet directly to confirm current services and costs and for details of other IEunet services: Email Casual Access, ISDN high speed access, 32K analogue leased line access, FTP storage, Faxlink, Easylink.	Dial-up access to the Internet for a single system. Includes access to email, File Transfer, Telnet, Gopher, WWW, News. Price £50 registration, plus £5 per hour (peak) £2.50 per hour (off peak). £25 monthly minimum. Unlimited access £100 per month + VAT.
	Dial-up access for a Local Area Network: Price £100 registration, plus £6 per hour (peak) £3 per hour (off peak). £25 monthly minimum. Unlimited access £200 per month + VAT.
	64K Digital Leased Line: High bandwidth network feed. Price £1000 setup, plus £5000 per year + VAT. You also need a router (approx. £1400) and a leased line from Telecom Eireann, (approx. £3000) and will pay TE rental costs (distance dependent, 1–5 miles £1000–2500).
	Web Space: Place your own Web pages on the IEunet Web Server. Price for one A4 page (approx. 40k size) £125 per year + VAT (not including cost of creating the Web pages).
Contact	IEunet, 34A Westland Square, Pearse Street, Dublin 2 Tel: (01) 6790832 email: *info@ieunet.ie*

Internet Eireann

Internet Eireann is based in Dublin. It offers full access to the Internet, seven-day telephone support, and a flat rate charge with no limits for time online or data transferred. It offers World Wide Web and consultancy services. Internet Eireann was founded in August 1994.

←B15
Who provides access?

←C11
So how does it all work?

Services offered and Costs (Oct 1995) Contact Internet Eireann directly to confirm current services and costs and for details of other services not listed here.	Standard Dial-up: Put a single computer on the Internet, with full connectivity — email, Usenet newsgroups, Gopher, File Transfer, Telnet, World Wide Web. Price £15 setup, plus £10 per month + VAT for unlimited access.
	Network Connection by Dedicated Dialup: A modem and phone line is reserved for the customer. Connection may be dialup or leased from Telecom Eireann by customer choice. Price £750 setup, plus £100 per month + VAT.
	64K Digital Leased Line: High bandwidth network feed. Price £1000 setup, plus £5000 per year + VAT. You also need a router (approx. £1400) and a leased line from Telecom Eireann, (approx. £3000) and will pay TE rental costs (distance dependent, 1–5 miles £1000–2500).
	Web Space: Place your own Web pages on the Internet Eireann Web Server. Price £1 per MB (approx twenty A4 pages) per month + VAT (not including cost of creating the pages).
Contact	Internet Eireann, Gardiner House, 64-66 Lower Gardiner Street, Dublin 1 Tel: (01) 2781060 email: *sales@internet-eireann.ie*

Ireland On-Line

Ireland On-Line, based in Galway and Dublin, offers full access to the Internet, online support, and a sales and consultancy service. It has local dial-up numbers in Dublin, Galway, Cork, Limerick and Sligo, with further access planned for other major population areas, as well as Northern Ireland.

← B15
Who provides access?

← C11
So how does it all work?

Services offered and Costs (Oct 1995) Discounts: basic subscription is £100 per year and advanced subscription is £200 per year if paid in advance. Contact Ireland On-Line directly to confirm current services and costs, and for details of services not listed here.	Basic Subscription: Unlimited login time with email, newsgroups (Usenet, Clarinet & IOL), Gopher, File Transfer, World Wide Web, plus 1MB personal disk storage space. Price £25 setup, plus £10 per month + VAT.
	Advanced Subscription: As above, plus Static IP Address, your own email domain (e.g. *jsoap@soap.iol.ie*) and a one page Web site. Price £25 setup, plus £20 per month + VAT.
	Network Connections: Range of prices, contact Ronan Mullally at IOL for current details.
	64K Digital Leased Line: Price £500 setup, plus £4500 per year + VAT (£750 + £4950 outside Dublin) plus router and Telecom Eireann related charges (see pp. 151–152).
	Web Space: Price for one page £300 per year + VAT; for ten pages £1000 per year + VAT (not including cost of creating the pages).
Contact	Dublin: Ireland On-Line, 87 Amien Street, Dublin 2, Tel: (01) 8551739 Galway: Ireland On-Line, Furbo, Co. Galway Tel: (091) 592727 email: *info@iol.ie*

Regional Internet Service Providers

Cork Internet Services and Shannon Internet Services are joint ventures involving IEunet — see separate entry on IEunet.

Eirenet operates independently in the Cork region.

Eirenet 4 Washington Street (2nd Floor) Cork (021) 274141 *sales@eirenet.net*	Put a single computer on the Internet, with full connectivity — £25 connection, plus £15 per month (basic service) or £30 per month (premium service) + VAT for unlimited access.
	ISDN dial-up, leased lines etc. — contact Eirenet directly for details.

HomeNet

HomeNet, the newest of the Irish Internet Service Providers, was launched just as this book was going to print. A subsidiary of the Horizon Computer group, HomeNet offers unlimited direct dial-up access for single users plus seven-day telephone support.

HomeNet PO Box 4892, Freepost Dublin 8 (01) 6716313 *ciara.griffin @horizon.ie*	Put a single computer on the Internet, with full connectivity — £25 connection, plus £12.50 per month (incl. VAT) for unlimited access.
	Discounts: the £25 connection fee includes the first month's access. If you pay your first year in advance, there is no connection fee.

Internet Service Providers in Northern Ireland

The Genesis Project offers standard dial-up access for £12.50 connection, plus £10 per month + VAT. They can be contacted at (01232) 560552.

Other UK-based Internet Service Providers accessible from Northern Ireland include: BTnet (01442) 295828; ElectricMail (01223) 501333; and EUnet GB (01227) 266466.

The URL File	**The Spirituality Page — http://www.protree.com/Spirit.html**

Look before you leap

There are various places where you can try out the Internet yourself before deciding whether or not to get online. The most obvious, and often the most useful, is to find a friend who is already online, and ask him or her to show you how it all works. Failing that, you can go to....

←B15
Who provides access?

←C11
So how does it all work?

ILAC Centre Library, Dublin

What you can do	If you have a library card, you can book to use the Net for two hours a week at the Library's Learning Resource Centre. You can surf through Web pages or use Telnet to access other computers, but you cannot use email. A users group has been set up to evaluate how best the Library service can use the Net.
Contact	Learning Resource Centre, ILAC Library, ILAC Centre, Dublin 1 Tel: (01) 8734333 email: *dubclib@iol.ie*

Cyber Cafés & other access points

What you can do	You can also access the Net on a pay-per-hour basis from a growing number of private members clubs, cyber-cafés and other businesses. There may also be a membership fee.
Contact	Internet HQ, 3–4 Crowe Street, Dublin 2 Further details: Patrick Woods (088) 619621 Internet Exchange, Dublin Further details: Barry Breslin 4758788 Cafe Bleu, Dun Laoghaire (planning move to new premises). Further details: Kieran O'Flaherty 2846550 Frontier Communications, 4 Bridge Street, Cork Further details: John Meade: (021) 551193

Sports Library — http://www.atm.ch.cam.ac.uk/sports/sports.html | The URL File

What does a modem do?

← B16
What you
need to
get online

← C11
So how
does it all
work?

A modem translates the digital signals (bits and bytes) that are generated by your computer into analogue signals (sound waves) that can be transmitted down the telephone line. At the other end, another modem translates the analogue signals back into digital signals, so that your message can be understood by the computer at that end.

Generally speaking, most reputable manufacturers will supply you with a modem that will work just as well any other modem you might have chosen. You can also buy cheap modems, and these will in all likelihood work reasonably well. However, as with many things in life, the less you pay for your modem, the less you can expect in terms of reliability and back-up. Also, an external modem may not work properly on a pre-pentium PC, depending on the type of serial port.

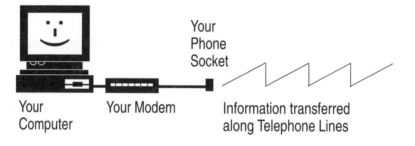

Your
Phone
Socket

Your
Computer

Your Modem

Information transferred
along Telephone Lines

What else should a good modem do?

Telephone lines have to comply to a certain level of quality for voice transmissions. However, there is often static and other interference on an average telephone line. Most modems have error correction capabilities to overcome this line noise. Most modems also include compression capabilities. This means they can compress files into a smaller amount of space before they transmit them. A good modem will comply with whatever is the current standard method of transmitting information by modem. Using this standard, a fast modem (14,400 bps) will be labelled *v.32 bis* on the outside of its box.

The URL File | **Stars and Galaxies — http://www.eia.brad.ac.uk/btl/**

Modem speeds on analogue telephone lines

The speed of your modem is measured in bps, or bits per second. A very slow modem will transmit 2,400 bits per second. A fast modem will transmit 28,800 bps. You can get even faster speeds — up to 56,000 bps — if your software will compress the files before transmitting them. Here are some examples of how these speeds (should) translate into real life.

←B16
What you
need to
get online

←C11
So how
does it all
work?

To put them into context, have a look at the files that you have stored on your own computer and see what size they are.

Modem Speed ...	2,400	9,600	14,400	28,800	56,600
a 2 kb email letter takes	7 sec	2 sec	1.2 sec	0.6 sec	0.3 sec
a 300 kb graphic image takes	16 min	4 min	3 min	1.5 min	45 sec
a 600 kb audio file takes	32 min	8 min	6 min	3 min	1.5 min
a 5 mb video file takes	5 hrs	70 min	50 min	25 min	12 min

Higher speed connections and ISDN

The first four of the above speeds (up to 28,800 bps) are based on modems that are transmitting information across normal analogue telephone lines. Higher speeds are possible with a dedicated connection that uses digital telephone lines instead. Because these lines already use digital information, you don't need a modem to translate your computer's digital signals into analogue signals for the phone lines.

ISDN, or Integrated Services Digital Network, can give you a digital telephone line divided into two bearer channels of 64,000 bps each. Using both simultaneously, you can get speeds of 128,000 bps. This technology is changing fast. If you think you may be interested in investing in ISDN, you should investigate how it is developing as well as what it can offer now.

Stereograms — http://mphh2.ph.man.ac.uk/gareth/sirds.html | The URL File

Software that you need to get online

You may need up to three types of software to use the Internet.

← B16
What you need to get online

1. Communications software to enable your computer to contact your Access Provider's computer in the first place.	This software should come with your modem. It allows your computer to act as if it were a terminal on the computer you have dialled.
2. Software to enable your computer to follow the protocols (or communication guidelines) that are used by other Internet computers.	This will typically include either SLIP or PPP software to allow your computer to act as if it were directly attached to the Internet. It does this by establishing a TCP / IP connection over the phone line.
3. Applications software to translate the noise coming down your phone line into pretty pictures on your computer screen.	For all of the things you want to do on the Internet (email, file transfer, Web etc.), you need specific applications software.

← C11
So how does it all work?

Software you can download once you are online

→ D15

Once you are actually online, you can download almost all of the applications software you need from the Internet itself. Much of it will typically be stored on your Service Provider's computer.

For most Internet application software, there is typically a free version that you can download to use basic functions, and a commercial version that allows you to use advanced features. With most applications, you can do most of what you need to do quite satisfactorily using the free versions.

Communications software

Communications software is what allows your computer to dial up another computer, and then use programmes on that other computer. You will generally get communications software with your modem. Any communications software that supports *VT-100 (ANSI) terminal emulation* will work as well as you need it to. Some common examples are..

←B16
What you need to get online

←C11
So how does it all work?

DOS	DOS or Windows	Macintosh
BLAST Pro	Hyperterm	Dynacomm
QModem	Telix	MacBLAST
QuickLink	Terminal	MicroPhone II
Smartcom	Crosstalk	Smartcom II
Telix	Comit	White Knight
Comit	Procomm Plus	WireTap
	Relay Gold	ZTerm

Internet protocol software

For full access, you will also need software to enable your computer to follow the protocols used by other computers on the Internet. This will include SLIP (Serial Line Internet Protocol) software or PPP (Point-to-Point Protocol) software.

You have to use whichever of these is supported by your Internet Service Provider's computer. SLIP is the older of the two, and is more widely supported. If your Provider gives you the option of which protocol to use, PPP is newer, and easier to use.

For SLIP or PPP with Windows you will need	For SLIP or PPP with Macintosh you will need
Winsock software, e.g.	MacTCP (included with System 7.5 or later)
Microsoft TCP/IP stack	
Trumpet Winsock	and either MacPPP
Chameleon	or InterSLIP

'The speed of the Web is inversely proportional to how many people you are demonstrating it to'

— *Andrew Blackburn*

Home Pages ▶

Section A ▶

Section B ▶

Section C ▶

Section D ▶ Information that
you will find useful
while or after you
get yourself online

The Ten Commandments of Netiquette ...

← C1
Electronic mail and talk

← C2
Mailing lists, news groups and chat

1 **Thou shalt keep thy email messages short whenever possible.** This is to save the system from being clogged up with a hundred million long messages every day.

2 **If thou hast to send a long message, don't worry about it.** Just try to use short messages rather than long ones if either option can get across the point you are conveying.

3 **Thou shalt use accurate, concise subject lines when composing email.** This helps whoever you are sending it to, when they are sorting out which emails to read first.

4 **If thou wants to convey emotion in thy email, use smileys (or emoticons).** These are little smiling or frowning faces which you read by looking at them sideways   :-)   :-(:-O

5 **If thou wants to add emphasis to a word or phrase, place understrokes like _this_ before** and after the word or phrase. Do _not_ use CAPS for emphasis (see No. 6).

... The Ten Commandments of Netiquette

← C1
Electronic mail and talk

← C2
Mailing lists, news groups and chat

6

THOU SHALT NOT TYPE IN ALL CAPS AS PEOPLE SHALL INTERPRET THIS AS SHOUTING AND SHALL PROBABLY FILL YOUR MAILBOX WITH ANGRY JUNK MAIL.

7

Thou can, if thou wishes, save time and space by using recognised abbreviations like BTW (by the way), IMO (in my opinion), IOW (in other words), NRN (no reply needed).

8

Thou shalt quote from other people's email where appropriate. Don't just send a reply to someone saying "I agree". First quote the piece from her email that you are agreeing with.

9

Thou shalt quote sparingly. This is part of "Keeping Thy Emails Short". Don't quote the whole message when replying, just extract the specific point you are replying to.

10

Thou shalt not get too upset about email thou doth not agree with. Chances are you'll only upset yourself rather than change the behaviour of the person who sent it.

Using smileys or emoticons

When speaking, you can smile or frown or change your tone of voice or punch somebody on the nose for emphasis. However, with email, it's just words. Your recipient, unaware that you are in fact the funniest person in Europe, may misinterpret your sarcasm as offensive abuse. To minimise the chances of this happening, you can add smileys or emoticons. You type them using colons, dashes etc. and you read them by tilting your head to the left and looking at them sideways. Some examples...

← C1
Electronic mail and talk

← C2
Mailing lists, news groups and chat

:-)	Happy	:-&	Tongue Tied
;-)	Winking	:-9	Licking Lips
:-D	Laughing	:-*	Kiss
:-(	Sad	:-I	Unimpressed
:'-(	Crying	=:-)	Punk
:-V	Shouting	0:-)	Saint
:-@	Screaming	8-)	Glasses
:-O	Shocked	I-)	Asleep

Some people with a lot of free time have composed directories of hundreds of somewhat less practical smileys, such as...

B-)	Batman	5:-J	Elvis Presley
I-]	Robocop	:-)=	Dracula
8)	Frog	)	Chesire Cat

Using TLAs

← C1
Electronic mail and talk

← C2
Mailing lists, news groups and chat

To save time when typing email, and to make your messages a little shorter, you can use what are known as TLAs or *Three Letter Acronyms*. If you are steeped in the traditions of mathematics and linguistics, you may notice that many have more than three letters and few are actually acronyms, but that's the Internet for you. You don't have to use TLAs, but you'll probably see them in other emails and want to be able to make sense of them.

AFAIK	As far as I know	**ITRW**	In the real world
AIUI	As I understand it	**LOL**	Laughing out loud
BST	But seriously though	**NFWM**	No flipping way, man
BTW	By the way	**NRN**	No reply needed
F2F	Face to face	**ROTFL**	Rolling on the floor laughing
FAQ	Frequently asked question	**RSN**	Real soon now
FFS	For flip's sake	**RTFM**	Read the flipping manual
FOC	Free of charge	**TIA**	Thanks in advance
FWIW	For what it's worth	**TIC**	Tongue in cheek
FYI	For your information	**TPTB**	The powers that be
IMO	In my opinion	**TVM**	Thanks very much
IMHO	In my humble opinion	**VC**	Virtual community
IOW	In other words	**VR**	Virtual reality
ISTM	It seems to me	**WRT**	With regard to

Ten More Commandments of Netiquette ...

← C1
Electronic mail and talk

← C2
Mailing lists, news groups and chat

1 **Thou shalt lurk before posting.** This is not a rude word. It refers to reading the contents of a mailing list or newsgroup for a while before sending anything to it.

2 **Thou shalt read the FAQ before posting.** FAQ means Frequently Asked Question(s) about a topic. If a FAQ document exists for a newsgroup, it should be posted about once a month or so.

3 **Thou shalt post to the appropriate mailing list or newsgroup only.** In particular, don't send commercial posts (i.e. advertisements) to non-commercial lists or groups.

4 **Thou shalt not spam.** Spamming refers to sending multiple copies of the same post to inappropriate newsgroups. It's a good way of clogging up your mailbox with angry replies.

5 **Thou shalt reply privately where relevant.** If you are replying to a question someone asked, consider whether to send your reply by private email or publicly to the list or newsgroup.

The URL File | **Thesaurus (Roget's) — http://wilma.cs.city.ac.uk/text.roget/thesaurus.html**

... Ten More Commandments of Netiquette

6

Thou shalt respect the privacy of private email. Don't publicly quote from a personal email message unless you have the permission of the person who sent it to you.

7

Thou shalt respect copyright. Or thou shalt end up in prison. Or at least paying a fine. Well, okay, you probably won't, but someday soon someone will be made a big example of here.

8

Thou shalt ignore chain letters and get-rich-quick pyramid schemes. You'll see them every so often on whatever mailing list or newsgroup you subscribe to. Ignore them.

9

Thou shalt beware of trolls. Trolls are posts designed specifically to be provocative. If you want to reply, sure, go ahead and do so, but don't get too emotionally unhinged about it.

10

Thou shalt keep flames in perspective. A flame is an abusive post, often from an utter ignoramus. Relax and consider rationally whether it is worth investing time in replying.

← C1
Electronic mail and talk

← C2
Mailing lists, news groups and chat

Note on *flame mail* (see No. 10) — if you find that somebody specific is repeatedly sending posts that you don't want to read, you can create a "kill file" that will prevent his or her messages from appearing on your computer.

Ten Top Gopher Sites ...

← C3
Information
on the
Internet

1 AskERIC

A compilation of subject information guides and lesson-planning aids to help educators; covers hundreds of topics.

Address:
ericir.
syr.edu

2 CMU's English Server

The server in Carnegie Mellon University's English department, this includes links to everything from classic novels to educational dissertations.

Address:
english.server.
hss.cms.edu

3 Electronic Frontier Foundation

The EFF aims to protect the rights of users of new technology, and has excellent freedom of information type data on its archives.

Address:
gopher.
eff.org

4 Electronic Newsstand

Includes archive material on hundreds of magazines and periodicals, tables of contents and descriptions of popular books, and a music CD catalogue.

Address:
gopher.
enews.com

5 Internic (Internet Network Info Centre)

Established by the National Science Foundation in the USA, this site contains lots of information on the Internet, especially for beginners.

Address:
gopher.
internic.net

... Ten Top Gopher Sites

← C3
Information
on the
Internet

6

Merit Network Information Centre

Loads of information on the Internet itself and how to use it, compiled by a consortium of public universities in Michegan, USA.

Address:
nic.merit.edu

7

University of Minnesota

The Home of The Gopher; best source of information on Gopher itself, including FAQs and technical, distribution and licensing details for Gopher software.

Address:
gopher.
tc.unm.edu

8

University of New Brunswick

Contains the FAQ (Frequently Asked Questions) files for all of the major categories of Usenet newsgroups, including the alt. category.

Address:
jupiter.sun.
csd.unb.ca

9

University of Southern California

Includes links to Gopher Jewels on community, government, health, law, personal development, research, technology and much more.

Address:
cwis.
usc.edu

10

US Government Information Service

One of the most comprehensive available sources of information on US government policy, legislation, supreme court opinions and much more.

Address:
eryx.syr.edu

Today's Cool Site — http://www.infi.net/cool.html

The URL File

Ten Top Web Sites for Information

← C3
Information on the Internet

1 Apple Computers

The home page of Apple Computers, with links to information about Apple products on both Web pages and Gopher sites.

Address:
http://www.apple.com

2 EINet galaxy

A guide to worldwide information and services, including public and commercial information plus services provided by EINet customers and affiliates.

Address:
http://galaxy.einet.net/galaxy.html

3 Electronic Frontier Foundation

The EFF aims to protect the rights of users of new technology. Its Web pages include an excellent guide to all aspects of using the Web.

Address:
http://www.eff.org

4 FutureNet

Over 8,000 regularly updated pages of news and entertainment — areas covered include world news, computing, video games, music and sport.

Address:
http://www.futurenet.co.uk

5 HealthNet

Provides a comprehensive set of links to medical and healthcare resources on the Internet, plus details on potential future healthcare applications.

Address:
http://debra.dgbt.doc.ca:80/~mike/healthnet

| The URL File | Tools for Windows — http://whiz.mfi.com:80/msj/ |

... Ten Top Web Sites for Information

← C3
Information
on the
Internet

6 Netscape's About The Internet Page

Links to various guides to what you can do on the Internet, a regularly updated Internet book list, and the home page of the Internet Society.

Address:
http://www.
netscape.
com/home/
about-the-
internet.html

7 PC Lube and Tune

Introductions, tutorials and education on various elements of PC hardware and software, including Internet software for Windows.

Address:
http://pclt.
cis.yale.edu/
pclt/default.
htm

8 Project Gutenberg

An ongoing project to put all the classics of literature onto the Web — so far includes Bronte, Dickens, Shakespeare, Shelley, Twain, Verne and more.

Address:
http://med-
amsa.bu.edu/
Gutenberg/
Welcome.html

9 US Library Of Congress

Includes links to exhibits and collections covering all aspects of American culture and history, plus Telnet access to the library's catalogue database.

Address:
http://lcweb.
loc.gov/
homepage/
lchp.html

10 Yahoo

The most comprehensive available directory of information available on the World Wide Web, subdivided into various categories.

Address:
http://www.
yahoo.com

Total Football — http://www.futurenet.co.uk/Forums/TotalFootball/

The URL File

Ten Top Anonymous FTP Sites ...

← C4
Down-
loading
files

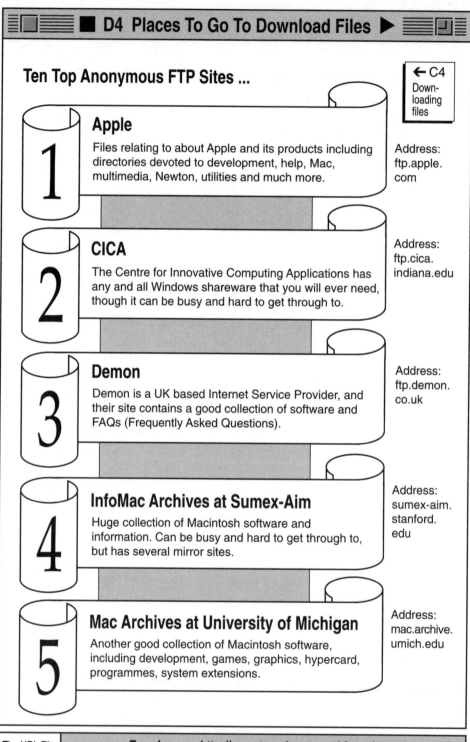

1

Apple

Files relating to about Apple and its products including directories devoted to development, help, Mac, multimedia, Newton, utilities and much more.

Address:
ftp.apple.
com

2

CICA

The Centre for Innovative Computing Applications has any and all Windows shareware that you will ever need, though it can be busy and hard to get through to.

Address:
ftp.cica.
indiana.edu

3

Demon

Demon is a UK based Internet Service Provider, and their site contains a good collection of software and FAQs (Frequently Asked Questions).

Address:
ftp.demon.
co.uk

4

InfoMac Archives at Sumex-Aim

Huge collection of Macintosh software and information. Can be busy and hard to get through to, but has several mirror sites.

Address:
sumex-aim.
stanford.
edu

5

Mac Archives at University of Michigan

Another good collection of Macintosh software, including development, games, graphics, hypercard, programmes, system extensions.

Address:
mac.archive.
umich.edu

The URL File | **Travelmag — http://www.travelmag.co.uk/travelmag**

... Ten Top Anonymous FTP Sites

← C4
Down-
loading
files

6 Microsoft

Information about Microsoft products, software updates and patches for Windows applications, plus resources for developers.

Address:
ftp.microsoft.
com

7 Scott Yanoff's Internet Service List

A comprehensive list of Internet services. The file that you want is called *inet.services.txt* and it is in a directory called *pub.*

Address:
ftp.csd.
uwm.edu

8 UUNET

Very large collection of Internet information, plus information on business, and the legislative, executive and judicial branches of US government.

Address:
ftp.uu.net

9 Washington University at St Louis

Loads of software for PCs running DOS and Windows, also acts as a mirror for the NCSA FTP site (National Center for SuperComputing Applications).

Address:
wuarchive.
wustl.edu

10 Your own Internet Service Provider

Most Internet Service Providers have their own FTP site, from which you can download files much more quickly than you can from external sites.

Address:
ask your
Service
Provider

UK Web Pages Index — http://www.ukindex.co.uk

The URL File

Ten Top Web Commercial Directories ...

← C5/6
Buying & selling on the Net

1

Avenue Commercial Profiles

A commercial service (i.e. you have to pay them) with up-to-date 5–15 page company profiles on more than 25,000 public, private and international companies.

Address:
http://www. avetech. com/avenue/ home.html

2

Directory Net

A large index of commercial sites hosted by Open Market Inc. Includes alphabetical listings and a search by keyword facility.

Address:
http://www. directory.net/

3

Industry Net

A US company whose page has links to information on new products, buying guides, online trade shows and an online newsletter, IndustryNet Daily.

Address:
http://www. industry.net/

4

International Business Resources

A listing maintained by Michigan State University, covers news/periodicals plus various international business resources and government resources.

Address:
http:// ciber.bus. msu.edu/ busres.htm

5

The Internet Mall

A free listing service for companies selling products and services through the Internet. Listings are also distributed through Usenet, email and Gopher.

Address:
http://www. mecklerweb. com/imall/

... Ten Top Web Commercial Directories

← C5/6
Buying & selling on the Net

6 Pathfinder

A Web site created by Time Inc. to help people to explore the Internet. Includes an interactive version of the Fortune 500 company listing.

Address: http://www. pathfinder. com/

7 UK Businesses On The Web

One of several UK business listings. Businesses are found by category or alphabetical listing. Covers computing, financial, industrial and retail sectors.

Address: http://www. u-net.com/ ukcom/

8 Web 100

Links to the largest US corporations on the Web today. It also gives an informative insight into the rapidly changing world of business on the Web.

Address: http://fox. nstn.ca/ ~at_info/ w100_intro. html

9 WWW Business Yellow Pages

Very comprehensive listing maintained by the University of Houston College of Business Adminis-tration. Includes a section for women on the Web.

Address: http://www. cba.uh.edu/ ylowpges/ ylowpges. html

10 Yahoo Directory Of Business Directories

Sort of says it all, really. From the main Yahoo page, go to *Business and Economy*, then to *Business Directory*, then to *Other Business Directories*.

Address: http://www. yahoo.com/

USA Today — http://www.usatoday.com/web1.htm

The URL File

My Personal Top Five Mailing Lists ...

To join these lists ..

1 Creativity & Creative Problem Solving

List address: *crea-cps@nic.surfnet.nl*

Busyish (approx. 100 posts a week) and friendly group discussing various aspects of creativity.

...send the message "sub crea-cps your name" to *listserv@ nic.surfnet.nl*

2 Humor — A Daily Digest of Jokes

List address: *humor@uga.cc.uga.edu*

Lighten up each day with about twenty or so jokes, at least some of which are usually funny.

...send the message "sub humor your name" to *listserv@ uga.cc.uga.edu*

3 League of Ireland Soccer

List address: *loisoccer@maths.tcd.ie*

Discuss League of Ireland and Irish national soccer, and how Irish players are performing abroad.

...send the message "sub loisoccer your name" to *loisoccer-request@ maths.tcd.ie*

4 Leeds United Supporters

List address: *leeds-united@vax.ox.ac.uk*

Very busy during the season, great fun — includes a prediction league and a related Web page.

...send the message "sub leeds-united your name" to *listserv@ vax.ox.ac.uk*

5 TIDBITS — A Newsletter for Mac Users

List address: *tidbits@ricevm1.rice.edu*

A very informative weekly newsletter on all aspects of Mac computers on the Net and in the real world.

...send the message "sub tidbits your name" to *listserv@ ricevm1. rice.edu*

The URL File | **Veterinary Resources — http://netvet.wustl.edu/**

My Personal Top Five Newsgroups ...

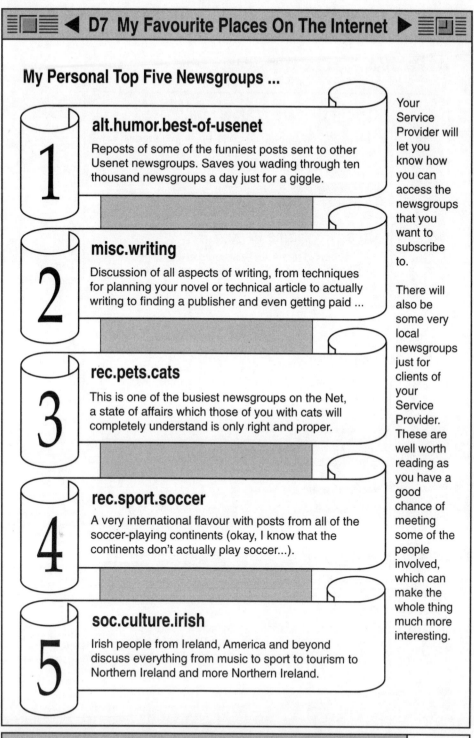

1 alt.humor.best-of-usenet

Reposts of some of the funniest posts sent to other Usenet newsgroups. Saves you wading through ten thousand newsgroups a day just for a giggle.

2 misc.writing

Discussion of all aspects of writing, from techniques for planning your novel or technical article to actually writing to finding a publisher and even getting paid ...

3 rec.pets.cats

This is one of the busiest newsgroups on the Net, a state of affairs which those of you with cats will completely understand is only right and proper.

4 rec.sport.soccer

A very international flavour with posts from all of the soccer-playing continents (okay, I know that the continents don't actually play soccer...).

5 soc.culture.irish

Irish people from Ireland, America and beyond discuss everything from music to sport to tourism to Northern Ireland and more Northern Ireland.

Your Service Provider will let you know how you can access the newsgroups that you want to subscribe to.

There will also be some very local newsgroups just for clients of your Service Provider. These are well worth reading as you have a good chance of meeting some of the people involved, which can make the whole thing much more interesting.

Viewmaster — http://www.teleport.com/~shojo/View/vm.html

The URL File

My Personal Top Five Web Sites ...

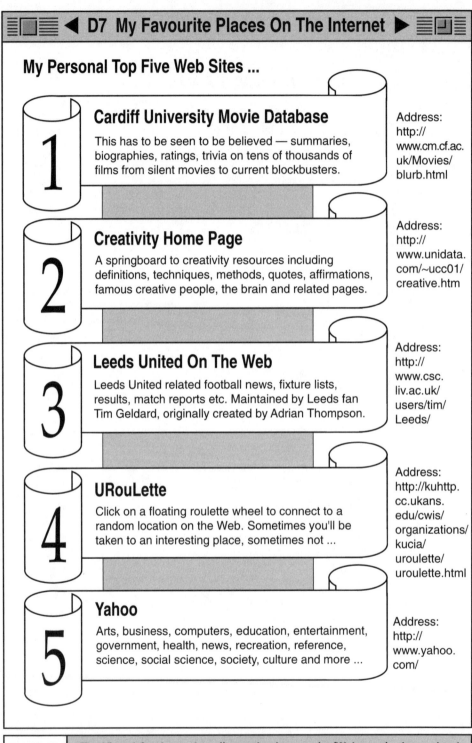

1

Cardiff University Movie Database

This has to be seen to be believed — summaries, biographies, ratings, trivia on tens of thousands of films from silent movies to current blockbusters.

Address:
http://
www.cm.cf.ac.
uk/Movies/
blurb.html

2

Creativity Home Page

A springboard to creativity resources including definitions, techniques, methods, quotes, affirmations, famous creative people, the brain and related pages.

Address:
http://
www.unidata.
com/~ucc01/
creative.htm

3

Leeds United On The Web

Leeds United related football news, fixture lists, results, match reports etc. Maintained by Leeds fan Tim Geldard, originally created by Adrian Thompson.

Address:
http://
www.csc.
liv.ac.uk/
users/tim/
Leeds/

4

URouLette

Click on a floating roulette wheel to connect to a random location on the Web. Sometimes you'll be taken to an interesting place, sometimes not ...

Address:
http://kuhttp.
cc.ukans.
edu/cwis/
organizations/
kucia/
uroulette/
uroulette.html

5

Yahoo

Arts, business, computers, education, entertainment, government, health, news, recreation, reference, science, social science, society, culture and more ...

Address:
http://
www.yahoo.
com/

| The URL File | **The Virtual Garden — http://www.timeinc.com/vg/Welcome/welcome.html** |

My Personal Top Five Web Search Pages ...

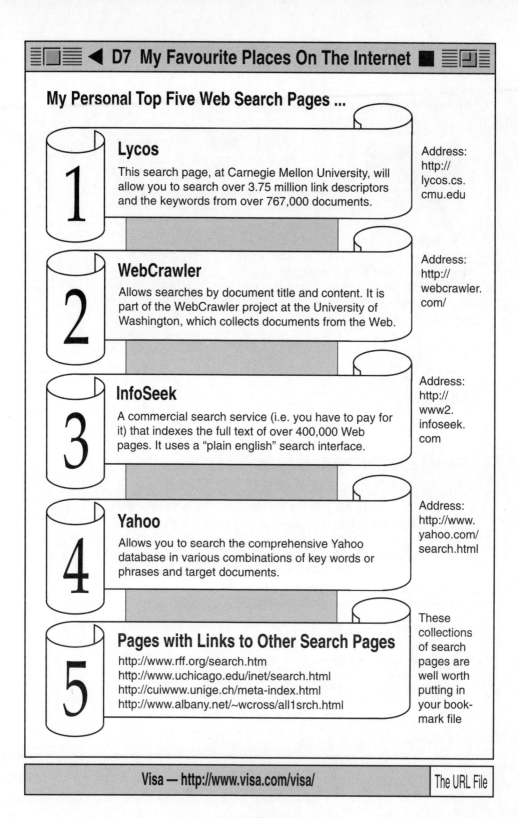

Lycos

1

This search page, at Carnegie Mellon University, will allow you to search over 3.75 million link descriptors and the keywords from over 767,000 documents.

Address:
http://
lycos.cs.
cmu.edu

WebCrawler

2

Allows searches by document title and content. It is part of the WebCrawler project at the University of Washington, which collects documents from the Web.

Address:
http://
webcrawler.
com/

InfoSeek

3

A commercial search service (i.e. you have to pay for it) that indexes the full text of over 400,000 Web pages. It uses a "plain english" search interface.

Address:
http://
www2.
infoseek.
com

Yahoo

4

Allows you to search the comprehensive Yahoo database in various combinations of key words or phrases and target documents.

Address:
http://www.
yahoo.com/
search.html

Pages with Links to Other Search Pages

5

http://www.rff.org/search.htm
http://www.uchicago.edu/inet/search.html
http://cuiwww.unige.ch/meta-index.html
http://www.albany.net/~wcross/all1srch.html

These collections of search pages are well worth putting in your bookmark file

Visa — http://www.visa.com/visa/   The URL File

Internet Eireann — who they are

← C15
Main Irish
Access
Providers

Internet Eireann is the pioneer of low cost full Internet access in Ireland. Started in August 1994 it is a wholly Irish family owned business. As well as standard dial-up access for the individual home or small business user with one computer, Internet Eireann provides a full range of Internet access options for medium to large businesses who want to connect their Local Area Networks to the Internet. The first service provider in Ireland to offer flat rate unlimited Internet access to our users — with no hidden extras for the amount of time spent online or amounts of information downloaded — Internet Eireann is dedicated to providing the best quality and value Internet connection possible. Internet Eireann connects to the rest of the world via the Sprint Global Network providing fast, high quality Internet access for our customers.

Steve O'Hara Smith — Managing Director, Internet Eireann

Internet Eireann— what they can do for you

Internet Eireann were the first Irish service provider to introduce PPP and SLIP access for £10 a month. Our aim is to provide a high quality of service and support at a competitive rate. Connections to the outside world are impressively fast. Users (and people evaluating the guest account) may avail of free, knowledgeable, all-week technical support. Every user is allocated a personal hostname (supporting multiple mail addresses) and a permanent IP address.

We encourage you to try our guest account and also those of other providers so you can fully appreciate our service. After your free use of our guest account, should you choose to subscribe to Internet Eireann on the basis of having bought this book, you will get a discount of 10% off your first subscription.

Dermot McNally — Technical Manager, Internet Eireann

| The URL File | **Volcano World — http://volcano.und.nodak.edu/** |

Your free Internet Eireann disk

This disk contains a selection of software to get you connected to the Internet. It comes preconfigured for our guest account, which you may access free for ten minutes at a time and which provides much of the functionality of a full account. With the increasing complexity of software, it is difficult to fit the best of everything onto a single disk, so we have provided the best selection possible in the space available — better and updated programmes are easily downloaded once connected, even from the guest account.

← C15
Main Irish Access Providers

← C16
Modems and software

Software	The disk contains a World Wide Web browser, an FTP (File Transfer) programme and the Eudora mail programme (only useable on a full account), and the Trumpet Winsock.
Installation	To install, follow the instructions printed on the disk. Please read the file README.TXT which provides more comprehensive and up-to-date information. While the setup programme will run on Windows 95, a more suitable means of connecting with Windows 95 is described in the file WIN95.TXT.
Macintosh Disk Exchange	You can exchange this PC disk, free of charge, for a disk with similar software for the Macintosh. Please telephone or call to Internet Eireann to make arrangements.

Note for Macintosh users with less than System 7.5 (which includes the protocol programme MacTCP) — you can purchase MacTCP directly from Apple, or with the "Internet Starter Kit For Macintosh" book (cost approx. IR£35).

Setup should be quick and painless — however, if problems do arise, or if you are unsure about a certain step, please feel free to call Internet Eireann technical support at (01) 8551724.

Note on free disks and discounts: the contents of pages 180–183 were provided by Internet Eireann and Ireland On-Line respectively. They are published in alphabetical order. In the experience of the author, both are companies who understand the complexities of Internet service provision and who are committed to providing comprehensive Internet access services for the Irish computer user.

WebMuseum: Bienvenue! — http://www.emf.net/louvre/	The URL File

Ireland On-Line — who they are

← C15
Main Irish
Access
Providers

Ireland On-Line was founded by Barry Flanagan in 1992 and began with a 286 laptop, a telephone line and a modem in the back room of Barry's home in Galway! From these modest beginnings Ireland On-Line has become Ireland's largest Internet Service Provider, with almost 6,000 users, over 200 dial-up lines nationwide, offices in Galway (Connemara) and Dublin and a staff of over 24 people. The objective of Ireland On-Line has always been to create an online community in Ireland and to provide online services with a particular focus on areas of Irish interest — a quick browse through the Ireland On-Line Home Pages will show that many Irish organisations and businesses are now using the World Wide Web to promote their services and to provide those services to Ireland On-Line users electronically. Rumours that the National Museum wish to acquire the original 286 laptop for display are exaggerated!

Ireland On-Line — what they can do for you

Ireland On-Line is Ireland's largest Internet Service Provider with almost 6,000 users at the time this book was going to print. This compares to approximately 300 users in March 1994 and 1000 users in November 1994 — a growth rate of 2000% in the past year and a half. Ireland On-Line was the first company to actively promote the Internet and on-line services to all computer users throughout the country. We have successfully managed to remove any mystique or complexity surrounding the Internet — users can use the Internet as easily as they can use any software on their computers. We also lead the way in encouraging organisations and businesses to provide information and services on Ireland On-Line — 2FM, Allied Irish Banks, CompuStore, IBEC, Premier Banking & Insurance and FÁS are examples of organisations who now use Ireland On-Line to promote themselves and provide services to on-line users.

Donal Harrington — Systems Manager, Ireland On-Line

The URL File	**Webster's Dictionary — http://c.gp.cs.cmu.edu:5103/prog/webster**

Your free Ireland On-Line disk

This disk contains software to connect to Ireland On-Line as a guest user. The guest account allows you to use the service for up to ten minutes at a time and allows you to view the entire Ireland On-Line site. If you would like to subscribe to Ireland On-Line and get unlimited access to the Internet, just follow the "subscribe" instructions on our Home Page. Should you subscribe on the basis of having bought this book, your first month's account with Ireland On-Line will be free of charge.

← C15
Main Irish Access Providers

← C16
Modems and software

Software	This disk includes an email programme, a Web browser which enables you to browse the World Wide Web, download files, etc., a Terminal Emulation programme and Internet protocol software.
Installation	To install the software, insert the disk in the drive, pick Run from the File menu, type "a:setup" and click the OK button — the setup programme will then lead you through the installation.
Macintosh Disk Exchange	You can exchange this PC disk, free of charge, for a disk with similar software for the Macintosh. Please telephone or call to Ireland On-Line to make arrangements.

Note for Macintosh users with less than System 7.5 (which includes the protocol programme MacTCP) — you can purchase MacTCP directly from Apple, or with the "Internet Starter Kit For Macintosh" book (cost approx. IR£35).

Once the software is installed you're ready to connect to Ireland On-Line. Should you have any problems with installation, or should you require any further information, please telephone Ireland On-Line at (01) 8551739.

Note on free disks and discounts: the contents of pages 180–183 were provided by Internet Eireann and Ireland On-Line respectively. They are published in alphabetical order. In the experience of the author, both are companies who understand the complexities of Internet service provision and who are committed to providing comprehensive Internet access services for the Irish computer user.

Weightlifting — http://www.cs.odu.edu/~ksw/weights.html | The URL File

Downloading PC applications software

Some places where you can download software (or updated versions of software that you already have) for use with a PC computer. Always first try the FTP site of your own Internet Service Provider, as local file transfers are much quicker and much more efficient in terms of Internet resources.

← B4
Down-loading files

← C16
Modems and software

← D4
Ten top FTP sites

Email for PCs	
Eudora	ftp.qualcomm.com ftp.red.net/pub/windows/comms/mail

Usenet news for PCs	
Winvn	ftp.cyberspace.com/pub/ppp/ windows/newsreaders

World Wide Web for PCs	
Netscape	ftp.netscape.com (the only site from which Netscape can be legally downloaded)
Mosaic	ftp.ncsa.uiuc.edu ftp.red.net/pub/windows/comms/

File Transfer for PCs	
Winftp	ftp.cyberspace.com/pub/ppp/windows/ftp

Archie for PCs	
WinArchie	ftp.cyberspace.com/pub/ppp/windows/archie

Gopher for PCs	
WinGopher	ftp.cyberspace.com/pub/ppp/windows/gopher

Telnet for PCs	
Telnet	ftp.ncsa.uiuc.edu/telnet/dos/

Your Service Provider should supply you with the applications software you need to get started on the Net in the first place.

Later you may want to try out different software.

When logging on to transfer files from these sites, type in *anonymous* as your username and your email address as your password.

Downloading Macintosh applications software

Some places where you can download software (or updated versions of software that you already have) for use with a Macintosh computer. Always first try the FTP site of your own Internet Service Provider, as local file transfers are much quicker and much more efficient in terms of Internet resources.

← B4
Down-
loading
files

← C16
Modems
and
software

← D4
Ten top
FTP sites

Email for Macintosh

Eudora	ftp.qualcomm.com ftp.red.net/pub/mac/comms/mail

Usenet news for Macintosh

Newswatcher	ftp.acns.nwu/edu/pub/newswatcher

World Wide Web for Macintosh

Netscape	ftp.netscape.com (the only site from which Netscape can be legally downloaded)
Mosaic	ftp.ncsa.uiuc.edu ftp.red.net/pub/windows/comms/www/

File Transfer for Macintosh

Fetch	ftp.dartmouth.com ftp.red.net/pub/mac/comms/ftp/

Archie for Macintosh

Anarchie	ftp.red.net/pub/mac/comms/ftp/

Gopher for Macintosh

Turbogopher	ftp.cyberspace.com/pub/ppp/mac/gopher

Telnet for Macintosh

Telnet	ftp.ncsa.uiuc.edu/

Your Service Provider should supply you with the applications software you need to get started on the Net in the first place.

Later you may want to try out different software.

When logging on to transfer files from these sites, type in *anonymous* as your username and your email address as your password.

Weirdness — http://phenom.physics.wisc.edu/~shalizi/hyper-weird/   The URL File

Index of main topics covered in this book

Further reading — other Irish-published books

The Ireland Guide to the Internet	Self-published in October 1995 by *Irish Independent* journalist Jim Aughney and Everyman Computer owner Jimmy Plenderleith; the first Irish-published book about the Internet.
	216 pages, price IR£9.95 Urban Dynamics, Drumcondra, Dublin ISBN 0-95268-470-5

The URL File	**Wine Net — http://desires.com/wine/index.html**

Further reading — Irish newspapers and magazines

The Irish Times Mondays	The *Computimes* page, edited by Fiachra Ó Marcaigh and Michael Cunningham, with up to a dozen regular contributors. Full page of comprehensive updates on the computer and Internet worlds with an emphasis on end-users rather than industry. *http://www.irish-times.ie/* *Email: computimes@irish-times.ie*
The Evening Herald Saturdays	*The Internet Column*, edited by Brendan Munnelly. Eclectic mix of Internet information, written in a short and snappy style. *Email: herald@independent.internet-eireann.ie*
Sunday Papers	❏ *The Sunday Business Post* — technology features by Carrisa Casey. At time of writing considering a regular Internet column. *Email: sbp@iol.ie* ❏ *The Sunday Times* — Internet features in the *Innovation* pages. *Email: innovation@delphi.com*
Computer Magazines	Most computer magazines have regular features on the Internet, including (published in Ireland) — ❏ *PC Live* (every two months, 52 pages, IR£1.95, by Computerscope Ltd). *Email: pclive@scope.ie* (Web site also planned for late 1995) ❏ *Irish Computer* (monthly, 56 pages, IR£1.70, by Computer Publications of Ireland). *Email: mccolgan@irish-computer.ie*

Electronic Frontier Ireland (see entry in Irish Web page directory) have published a useful booklet containing a simple guide to how the Internet works, and how to get connected to it. It can be obtained by sending a stamped addressed envelope to The Secretary, Electronic Frontier Ireland, 28, Charleston Avenue, Dublin 6, or online at the EFI home page at *http://www.maths.tcd.ie/~efi*

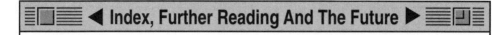

Further reading — recommended UK Internet magazines

.net 116 pages, IR3.85 (UK£2.95)	Monthly by Future Publishing. Sample articles and writers: Artists show off in cyberspace; Times and trials of a Net newbie; Secret life of email; Richard Longhurst, Davey Winder, Cotton Ward, Ivan Pope. *http://www.futurenet.co.uk/net.html* *Email: netmag@futurenet.co.uk*
.net Directory 196 pages, IR£6.45 (UK£4.99)	Every two months by Future Publishing. Directory to "guide you, chide you and baby-mind you through the familiar delirium of information overdose". *http://www.futurenet.co.uk/computing/netdirectory.html* *Email: alowe@futurenet.co.uk*
Internet 132 pages, IR£3.30 (UK£2.50)	Monthly by Emap Computing. Sample articles and writers: ISDN explained; Slash your Internet costs; Women get wired; Let Archie find that file; Neil Ellul, Paul Lavin, Daniel Dern, Ivan Pope. *http://www.emap.co.uk/comp/magazines/internet/* *Email: internet@computing.emap.co.uk*
Internet & Comms Today 100 pages, IR£3.85 (UK£2.95)	Monthly by Paragon Publishing. Sample articles and writers: Terminal addiction; Cutting your modem bills; Education and the Net; Dave Westley, Joel Furr, Jack Schofield; How to design Web pages. *http://www.paragon.co.uk/ict/home.html* *Email: ict@paragon.co.uk*
Net User 132 pages, IR£5.15 (UK£3.95)	Every two months by Paragon Publishing. Directories and reviews of what's new on the Internet, plus articles for beginner to intermediate level Net users. *http://www.paragon.co.uk/neu/netuser.html* *Email: ict@paragon.co.uk*
The Web 132 pages, IR£3.30 (UK£2.50)	Every two months by IDG Media; first issue appeared just as this book went to print. Wide range of articles and very comprehensive Web page listing guide. *http://www.idg.co.uk/theweb* *Email: theweb@idg.co.uk*

The URL File	**World Bank — http://www.worldbank.org**

Further reading — recommended reference books for detailed information on using Internet programmes

To build on the general overview of the Internet provided by this book, I recommend that you buy at least one of those enormous books that look ridiculously expensive but are actually excellent value for money if you want to have a detailed reference book to hand when learning your way around the Net. Of the many such books I have read in researching *Ireland On The Internet,* the two I recommend most are:

Special Edition Using The Internet	Astonishingly comprehensive users guide written by Mary Anne Pike with a host of expert specialist contributors on all aspects of using the Internet. Includes a free CD with software and information files. 1250 pages, price IR£37.49 (US$39.99) Que Corporation ISBN 0-7897-0077-8
The Internet Starter Kit for Macintosh	Very comprehensive start-up guide with free software (including MacTCP) and step-by-step instructions for using essential Internet programmes. By Adam C. Engst, publisher of the email newsletter TidBits. 990 pages, price IR£35 (US$29.95) Hayden Books, Macmillan Computer Publishing ISBN 1-56830-111-1

You might also consider buying *net.speak* — *The Internet Dictionary*, a comprehensive A–Z reference of over 2,000 essential Internet terms (212 pages, price IR£14.40 (US$15), Hayden Books, ISBN 1-56830-095-6)

Like anything else, the more you read about something — and the more you actually use it — the more comprehensively you will understand it. While the basics of the Internet are clearly outlined in this book, there are unlimited levels of extra detail. Often by reading about the same thing from different perspectives, you will form your own "aha" style understanding of exactly what is being explained. The best combination is regular use of the Internet and regular reading of the most up-to-date information on the areas of the Internet you find yourself using most often.

World Health Organisation — http://www.who.ch/Welcome.html | The URL File

◀ Index, Further Reading And The Future ▶

The future of the Internet

The reality of the Internet — the organised chaos of an evolving communications system — does not meet the Utopian standards boasted about by the Net evangelists who view it through rose-tinted computer screens. Nor did the reality of the motor-car, the telephone or the television at the early stages of their introduction to the general public. Stephen Fry has compared the Internet to an adolescent — growing rapidly, voice getting deeper, behaviour unpredictable, seeking greater independence, and constantly bursting out in facial eruptions. Using this anology, the Internet will mature in a matter of years. Unfortunately, we do not yet know what it will be when it grows up.

Many important Internet-related debates will be resolved only by time. What will be the impact on the Internet of the recent involvement of the major Online Commercial Services such as CompuServe and America On-Line? Who will set the software standards for online communication — Netscape or Microsoft, or another new challenger? Will every online transaction put another few cents into Bill Gates' bank account? Will Al Gore's proposed Information Superhighway become a reality? What will happen when the technology allows large-scale images and sound to be transmitted fast enough to satisfy the television-reared consumer?

Finally — the ultimate test of when the Internet has matured — when will the media stop producing misleading and sensationalist features about online credit card fraud and pornography?

A conversation sometime in the future about why it just didn't work out as it was planned...

Smiley   Well, that was a nice meal. Now where were we? Oh yes, I was saying — it's a shame it didn't work out. I mean, at the time it all started, people were convinced it was the communications medium of the future...

Wise   *It never had a chance. Just look at the problems it had to overcome. You could never tell who you were communicating with — you'd send your credit card number to somebody and you'd never know whose hands it might end up in.*

| The URL File | Yoga — http://www.genius.net/indolink/Health/yoga.html |

Waiter   Your bill, sir.

Wise   Thank you, my good man. Here's my credit card.

Waiter   Thank *you*. I'll be off into a back room where you can't see what I'm doing with your card.

Wise   Ermmm... that's fine. Very safe. Now, where was I?

Smiley   Credit card fraud.

Wise   And that's not all. Despite all the hype, it was a chaotic and slow process to find any useful information.

Smiley   Where did you hear that?

Wise   I read it somewhere. A statistic about how slow it is to locate information. It's in this book, I think. Yes, here it is, it says — hold on, I'll find it in a minute — or was it in that other book — no, I wrote it down in my diary — well, I'll find it soon, but that's not all anyway. There was a survey that showed that 80% of the messages communicated were pornography related...

Smiley   That's right — they surveyed the particular places that people used to transmit pornography. Not surprisingly, they found a high proportion of pornography there. But didn't the same survey show that, taking the system as a whole, the proportion of pornographic messages was less than half of one percent?

Wise   Sure, yeah, but where's the headlines in that? Anyway, that wasn't all. I mean, anybody could use it to transmit information. It was impossible for governments to effectively control it....

Smiley   Well, that says it all, really — unsafe, slow to find information, containing pornography, and impossible for governments to effectively control. Despite all the hype at the time it started, printing was *never* going to be the medium of the future.

Wise   You're right. I'll check up that statistic on the Internet when I get back to the office, and I'll email it to you. By the way, have you seen that waiter chappie? He's been gone quite some time with my credit card — Waiter !!!!!!

Smiley   And put that book away before he comes back — you don't want him to think you're a geek.

The Electronic Zoo — http://netvet.wustl.edu/e-zoo.html | The URL File

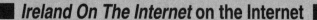
Ireland On The Internet Web pages

A series of *Ireland On The Internet* Web pages, which are in the planning stage and due for launch in 1996, will include updates to the information in this book and will be accessible to readers who have bought this book. The planned address for these pages is *http://www.nugent.ie/ireland-internet/*. If you would like me to send you further up-to-date information on this facility — or if you have any comments or suggestions for possible future editions of *Ireland On The Internet* — please email me at

mnugent@internet-eireann.ie or *mnugent@iol.ie*

Changes to listed Web page addresses

As the Web is continually evolving, some of the addresses (or URLs) listed in this book may have changed or expired since the book went to print. If this happens, try the following steps:

(1) Try deleting the last part of the address (to the most recent "/" — e.g. if you cannot get access to the file *http://www.xyz.ie/files/pageone*, try *http://www.xyz.ie/files/* instead. This should bring you to the next directory up from the page you are looking for. From there, you can check if there is any other way of getting to the page you want. If that doesn't work, go back to the next most recent "/" — *http://www.xyz/* and see where you can go from there.

(2) Try using one of the World Wide Web search facilities listed on page 179 of this book. Use different variations of key words likely to be included in the page you are looking for. Even if you can't find the page, you will find a selection of other pages on the same topic.

(3) Ask by sending an email to the email address, if one is listed. That is less likely to have changed. If there is no email address, try sending an email to the Internet Service Provider, if you can figure out their name from the Web page address (try *postmaster@the.address* or *webmaster@the.address*).

(4) If all else fails, please email me and I will try to assist you. Please also email me with details of any changes or new URLS — particularly Irish or Irish-related ones.

The URL File	*Ireland On The Internet* Web pages — See panel above for details